《文部科学省後援》

技術英検
2級問題集

JMA 一般社団法人日本能率協会
JSTC技術英語委員会

技術英検2級（2020～2023）&【旧検定名称】工業英検3級（2019）過去15回分収録

2024年度版

JN006331

日本能率協会マネジメントセンター

技術英語とは

「技術英語」と聞くと、どのような内容の英語を想像するでしょうか。「難しい科学の文章が出るに違いない」、「学校の英語の授業で習った英単語だけでは合格できない」、「理系の人たち専用の試験」といったことではないでしょうか。しかし、そんなことはまったくありません。

技術英語にあたる英語は "Technical Communication (in English)"、また、ライティングのみを示すのであれば "Technical Writing (in English)" です。つまり、この「技術」というのは、科学のジャンルの1つである「テクノロジー」ではなく、「テクニカル・コミュニケーション」という「英語でのコミュニケーションの手法」がベースであるということを意味しています。

テクニカル・コミュニケーションについては、米国でもさまざまな定義があります。最新の定義をうまくまとめてある "Introduction to Technical and Professional Communication"（Brigitte Mussack 著）の定義を引用すると、「テクニカル・コミュニケーションは技術の説明に加え、専門的な内容を分かりやすく説明すること、読み手に行って欲しい内容を説明すること、ものの定義、指示、情報の提供、説得」と書かれています。そして「内容だけではなく、書き方も重要である」と追記しています。このような特徴があるために、論理的な物事の説明に向いているわけです。

テクニカル・コミュニケーションはもともと、装置やシステムの仕組みやマニュアルを説明するための手法として始まりました。しかし、今では業界や業種を超え、多くの企業や大学で推奨されています。異なる名称が付けられていることもありますが、テクニカル・コミュニケーションが提唱している3C（Clear, Concise, Correct）、そしてパラグラフ・ライティングと内容は変わりません。「物事を分かりやすく、正確に伝える」ということを追求していくと、自然とコミュニケーションの究極の形である3Cとパラグラフに辿り着くということでしょう。

本検定の各級に共通しているのは、英語力（テクニカル・コミュニケーションの力）があれば、理系、文系を問わず、どのようなバックグラウンドの方でも合格できる、という点です。科学の知識は必要とせず、あくまでも英語力が問われる試験となるように問題を作成しています。どの級も、常に最新で、読んでも面白い、一般的な科学、ビジネス分野から出題されます。各級を順番に合格していくことで、一般的な意味での英語力向上に加え、せっかく向上した英語力をどう有効的に使うか、という力も正しい順序で高めていくことができます。本検定の内容は、英語を実践的に使う際に大いに役立つでしょう。

技術情報の交流や輸出入が増えている現在、コミュニケーションの手段として、技術英語の正しい理解と活用が学界、産業界で必須のものとなっています。ぜひ本検定を通して、世界基準の英語力を身につけていただきたいと願っています。

〈工業英検から技術英検へ〉

本検定の事業母体であった公益社団法人技術英語協会（のちに解散、一般社団法人日本能率協会に事業移管）は、「科学技術文書を英語で読む能力、書く能力、話す能力、聞く能力を客観的に正しく評価する」ための資格検定試験として、1981年より「工業英語能力検定」を実施し、これまでに、工業高校・高等専門学校・大学等の生徒・学生や研究者、企業等において科学技術文書の作成や翻訳に携わる方々、翻訳専門会社の翻訳者など、数多くの方に受検をいただいてきました。

一方で、当初は、我が国の主要産業である「工業」を名称に掲げましたが、工業英語能力検定の核となるテクニカル・コミュニケーションが提唱する3C、およびパラグラフ・ライティングの考え方の有効性が実証されてくるにつれ、本国である米国では工業系にとどまらず、大半の企業、大学でテクニカル・コミュニケーションの手法を使った文書作成を推奨するようになりました。

このような状況を鑑み、本検定の一層の普及に向けて、令和2年度（2020年度）より本検定の名称を「工業英検／工業英語能力検定」から、テクニカル・コミュニケーションのより正確な訳となる「技術英検／技術英語能力検定」へと変更いたしました。本検定の目的や資格体系は現状を維持しつつ、よりわかりやすい名称へと変更することによって、理工系分野の方々のみならず幅広く訴求し、我が国のテクニカル・コミュニケーション力向上に寄与いたしたいと考えます。

〈技術英語の要となる"3C"の考え方〉

Clear（明確に）

- ✓ 1回読めば理解できる英文
- ✓ 伝えるべき内容の論理関係を明確にした英文
- ✓ 具体的で分かりやすい語句と構文を使った英文

Concise（簡潔に）

- ✓ できるだけ少ない語数で伝わる英文
- ✓ 簡潔でより直接的に表現した英文
- ✓ 読み手の負担を最大限減らした英文

Correct（正確に）

- ✓ 的確な名詞や動詞が使われている英文
- ✓ 文法ミスや数字の間違いのない英文

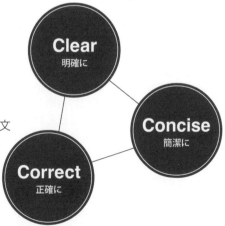

〈試験概要〉

受験資格

受験資格は一切ありません。どなたでも受験できます。

試験日

年3回実施（プロフェッショナルは年2回のみ実施）
＊詳細は下記ホームページをご確認ください。

試験形式

各級	出題形式	対象	団体受験
プロフェッショナル	記述式	科学・技術分野の英語文書を読みこなし、かつ正しく、明確に、簡潔に書くことができる。文書のスタイルは種類（マニュアル、仕様書、論文等）に応じて異なることを理解しており、正しく使いわけることができる。	×
準プロフェッショナル			
1級	選択式／記述式	科学・技術に関する英文を読むことができる。英文資料の要約、議事録、英文 E-mail 等の短文が書ける。	○
2級	選択式	科学・技術英語の語彙力があり、構文・文法を理解している。	○
3級	選択式	科学・技術英語の基礎的な語彙力があり、構文の基礎を理解している。	○

検定料 (公開会場料金／税込)

プロフェッショナル	準プロフェッショナル	1級	2級	3級
￥16,500		￥6,400	￥5,300	￥2,600

＊「プロフェッショナル」「準プロフェッショナル」は同一の問題となり、得点率に応じての判定となります。

〈技術英検2級出題内容〉 審査基準：合計で 60％ 以上の正解

No.	出題形式	問題数	配点	解答形式
Ⅰ	語彙（英→日）	10	20点	マークシート方式
Ⅱ	語彙（日→英）	10	20点	
Ⅲ	語彙解釈	4	20点	
Ⅳ	英文空所補充1	4	20点	
Ⅴ	英文空所補充2	8	40点	
Ⅵ	英文和訳	1	32点	
Ⅶ	英作文	6	48点	

一般社団法人日本能率協会
JSTC 技術英語委員会
Japan Society for Technical Communication
〒 105-0011 東京都港区芝公園 3-1-22
● TEL：03-3434-2350 　● E-mail：info@jstc.jp 　● HP：https://jstc.jma.or.jp

〈目次〉

技術英検 2 級試験問題ならびに工業英検 3 級試験問題

技術英検 2 級解答ならびに工業英検 3 級解答

※ 2020 年 5 月の第 123 回技術英語能力検定は、新型コロナウイルス感染拡大にともなう政府の緊急事態宣言を受け、中止いたしました。

技術英検
2級試験問題

ならびに工業英検3級試験問題

試験時間：70分

第 133 回（2023. 11）

I　次の（a）から（j）の各語について、（　）に入れるべき最適な語を選び、その番号を解答欄に記入にしなさい。

(a)　騒音低減
noise（　　）
1. reduction
2. low
3. flatness

(b)　高濃度
high（　　）
1. depth
2. rise
3. concentration

(c)　垂直線
（　　）line
1. horizontal
2. in
3. perpendicular

(d)　有害物質
（　　）material
1. worst
2. hazardous
3. harm

(e)　紫外線
（　　）rays
purple
2. ultraviolet
3. off violet

(f)　入力電圧
input（　　）
1. electricity
2. voltage
3. volcano

8

(g) 吸引力
(　) power
1. breathe
2. suction
3. return

(h) バッテリー容量
battery (　)
1. container
2. capacity
3. capability

(i) 人工知能
(　) intelligence
1. aided
2. acted
3. artificial

(j) 連鎖反応
(　) reaction
1. continue
2. automatic
3. chain

Ⅱ　次の (a) から (e) の英語の説明に対応する語を下の1から10より選び、その番号を解答欄に記入しなさい。なお、1から10は1回しか使えません。

(a) To make something work in the way that you want it to work

(b) A loud rumbling or crashing noise heard after a lightning flash due to the expansion of rapidly heated air

(c) Damage caused to water, air, etc. by harmful substances or waste

(d) A rod, wire, or other devices used to transmit or receive radio or television signals

(e) Any of a group of natural substances that are necessary in small amounts for the growth and good health of the body

1. oil	2. cloud	3. vitamin	4. control
5. sound	6. disease	7. pollution	8. thunder
9. like	10. antenna		

Ⅲ　次の (a) から (j) の英文を完成させる語として、最適なものをそれぞ
　　れの 1 から 4 より選び、その番号を解答欄に記入しなさい。

(a)　A steam engine uses heat to boil water (1. consumed　2. contained
　　3. consisted　4. confused) in a pressure vessel.

(b)　Oxygen is continuously (1. oriented　2. breathed　3. generated
　　4. aired) in the atmosphere through photosynthesis, which is a
　　process that uses sunlight as a source of energy.

(c)　Asteroids and comets can drive humans to (1. distinction
　　2. mitigation　3. duration　4. extinction) if they hit the earth.

(d)　(1. By　2. With　3. In　4. As) the world's population ages,
　　Parkinson's disease is impacting an increasing number of people.

(e)　The university has imposed (1. restorations　2. retirements
　　3. returns　4. restrictions) on the use of drugs such as morphine
　　in experiments.

(f)　In electronics, the transistor is known as the most (1. essential
　　2. burden　3. intentional　4. applicant) switching component.

(g)　This warranty does not apply to damage resulting from repairs or
　　(1. modifications　2. intact　3. termination　4. primitive) outside
　　of our authorized stores.

(h) Before the test, the research team carefully (1. refined 2. deduced　3. misfortune　4. formidable) the substance to remove all impurities.

(i) (1. However　2. What　3. Despite　4. Regardless of) the type of transmission, a car transmission is what moves the power from the engine to the wheels.

(j) Biodegradable plastics can be decomposed by microorganisms, and thus are (1. less　2. likely　3. expectably　4. look) harmful to the environment.

Ⅳ　次の (a) から (d) の各組の英文が同じ意味になるように、( ) に入れるべき最適な語を下の 1 から 10 より選び、その番号を解答欄に記入しなさい。なお、1 から 10 は 1 回しか使えません。文頭に来るべき語であっても先頭は小文字になっています。

(a)　If we can pay a company to do this process, we can save a lot of time.

(　　　　) this process should save us a lot of time.

(b)　The first commercial space project did not go well because the budget was not enough.

The failure of the first commercial space project was caused by (　　　　) funding.

(c)　The prices of pre-owned cars go up and down because they are dependent on supply and demand, which always change.

The prices of pre-owned cars are (　　　　) because their supply and demand always change.

(d) If a diamond has a natural color such as green, blue, or yellow, its value becomes much higher.

A naturally colored diamond has a significantly (　　　) value.

1. payment　　　2. insufficient　3. giving　　　4. unstable

5. greatly　　　6. best　　　7. up　　　　8. outsourcing

9. stable　　　10. enhanced

Ⅴ　次の (a) から (f) の英文がそれぞれ和文と同じ意味になるように、(　)
に入れるべき最適な語を下の 1 から 15 より選び、その番号を解答欄に
記入しなさい。なお、1 から 15 は 1 回しか使えません。文頭に来るべ
き語であっても先頭は小文字になっています。

(a) Our (　　　　) was that we would pay ¥5 more for each part; and in exchange, they would allow us to sell it exclusively.

私たちが達した妥協案は、それぞれのパーツを 5 円増しで買う
代わりに、販売の独占権を得る、というものでした。

(b) The software works almost the same as other similar products, but the (　　　) feature is that it is far easier to use.

このソフトウェアは他社の同様の製品と同じように動くが、特
徴的なのは、他社のものより圧倒的に簡単に使える、というこ
とである。

(c) We need to find the original document, because the duplicate was made before the writer (　　　) the original.

この書類のコピーは、作成者が元の書類を修正する前に取られ
たため、元の書類を探す必要がある。

(d)　When you are searching for papers related to your research theme, read their (　　　　　) first, because it saves time.

研究テーマに関連する論文を探すとき、まずは論文の要約文を読むようにすると時間の節約になります。

(e)　When you open the device, be very careful, because the battery acid might have (　　　　　) the inside of the device.

バッテリーの酸でこの機器の内部が腐食している可能性があるため、開ける際は気を付けなければならない。

(f)　With increasing (　　　　　　), carbon fiber is being used for this type of product to satisfy demands for strength and lightness.

丈夫さと軽さを求める声に応えるため、カーボンファイバーはこの種の製品にますます多く使われてきている。

1.　forecast　　　2.　compound　3.　detective　　4.　abstracts

5.　friction　　　6.　informed　　7.　coughed　　8.　compulsion

9.　revised　　　10. ability　　　11. frequency　12. distinctive

13. corroded　　14. reversed　　15. compromise

VI　次の英文を読んで、各設問に答えなさい。

There are approximately 500 active volcanoes in the world today, not including those underneath the oceans. <u>In fact, as you read these words, there are probably 20 volcanoes erupting right now.</u> Between 50-70 volcanoes are erupting every year, and 160 have erupted in the last decade. There are about 550 that have erupted since the beginning of recorded history.

The definition of an active volcano is difficult to pin down, since single volcanoes can have networks of volcanic vents across their flanks[*]. In Iceland, there can be eruptions (　①　) volcanic fields hundreds of kilometers long. At Mexico's Michoacan-Guanajuanto field, there are 1,400 cinder cones and shield volcanoes coming from a single magma chamber.

［注］*flank: 山腹

(a) 本文の英文に合うタイトルを次の 1 から 4 より選び、その番号を解答欄に記入しなさい。

1.　How to count the number of active volcanoes
2.　Active volcanoes around the world and the frequency of the eruptions
3.　Pinning down the active volcanoes from their networks
4.　Single magma chamber can erupt from many vents

(b) 下線部の和訳として最も適切なものを次の 1 から 4 より選び、その番号を解答欄に記入しなさい。

1.　事実上、これら 500 の火山のうちの 20 くらいが噴火していることになるだろう。
2.　実際、いまこれを読んでいる間にも、20 くらいの火山が噴火している。

3. 実際、これらの言葉を証明するかのように、20 くらいの火山が噴火している。

4. おそらく 20 くらいの火山が噴火しているが、それを事実として記録するのは難しい。

(c) （ ① ）に入る最も適切な語句を次の 1 から 4 より選び、その番号を解答欄に記入しなさい。

1. along
2. which
3. by
4. having

(d) 英文の内容と一致しているものを次の 1 から 4 より選び、その番号を解答欄に記入しなさい。

1. 今までの歴史上、550 の火山が噴火している。
2. 火山口から噴火しているものも 1 つの火山として考える。
3. メキシコだけでも 1,400 もの休火山があると言われている。
4. 昨年だけでも 160 の火山が噴火している。

Ⅶ 次の (a) から (f) について、各和文の意味を表すように 1 から 7 を並べかえて英文を作り、3番目と5番目にくる語の番号を解答欄に記入しなさい。

(a) その装置に直接触れるすべての部品は、ステンレス製でなければならない。

All parts (1. be　2. with　3. of　4. the equipment　5. made 6. in direct contact　7. must) stainless steel.

(b) このプリンターを設定するには、コンピューターに接続して電源を入れます。

To set up this printer, (1. and　2. your computer　3. it　4. plug 5. turn　6. into　7. on) the power.

(c) この現象は、入力電力がある値より大きい場合にのみ現れる。

This phenomenon appears (1. a　2. greater　3. when　4. than　5. is 6. the input power　7. only) certain value.

(d) 状況の変化に応じて、両社はライセンス契約を若干変更した。

The two companies modified their (1. response　2. changing 3. slightly　4. in　5. to　6. license agreement　7. the) situation.

(e) 職員の付き添いがなければ、訪問者は制御室には入れません。

Visitors are not (1. the control room　2. to enter　3. escorted 4. allowed　5. without　6. by　7. being) a staff member.

(f) 最近の研究では、水中騒音が鯨の聴力に直接害を与える可能性があることが示唆されている。

Recent studies (1. underwater noise　2. whales　3. can directly 4. that　5. suggest　6. by　7. harm) damaging their hearing.

第 132 回（2023.6）

I　次の（a）から（j）の各語について、（　）に入れるべき最適な語を選び、
その番号を解答欄に記入にしなさい。

(a) 異物
（　　）substance
1. foregoing
2. foreign
3. foreseen

(b) 回路図
circuit（　　）
1. diagonal
2. diagnosis
3. diagram

(c) 活断層
active（　　）
1. failure
2. fault
3. layer

(d) 磁束
magnetic（　　）
1. flux
2. flow
3. line

(e) 焦点距離
（　　）length
1. focalized
2. focalization
3. focal

(f) 静止軌道
（　　）orbit
1. stationer
2. stationing
3. stationary

(g)　定期点検
　　　(　　　) inspection
- 1. periodic
- 2. periodicity
- 3. permanent

(h)　二次方程式
　　　(　　　) equation
- 1. secondary
- 2. quadratic
- 3. bilateral

(i)　防湿の
　　　moisture-(　　　)
- 1. proof
- 2. optimal
- 3. disposable

(j)　確率分布
　　　(　　　) distribution
- 1. probation
- 2. probable
- 3. probability

Ⅱ　次の (a) から (e) の英語の説明に対応する語を下の 1 から 10 より選び、その番号を解答欄に記入しなさい。なお、1 から 10 は 1 回しか使えません。

(a) A straight line that connects two points on the circumference of a circle and passes through the center

(b) Our body's ability to use our defense system to avoid harmful substances or disease

(c) Materials such as rubber, wood, and plastic that have high resistance to the flow of electricity

(d) Property of being able to return to its original shape after being stretched or compressed

(e) The last part of a discourse, usually containing a summing up of the points

1. conclusion　2. diameter　　3. tensive　　4. elastic
5. arch　　　　6. insulators　7. neutron　　8. lymph nodes
9. immunity　　10. exclusion

Ⅲ　次の (a) から (j) の英文を完成させる語として、最適なものをそれぞ
れの 1 から 4 より選び、その番号を解答欄に記入しなさい。

(a)　An earthquake is the sudden release of (1. stress　2. steel
3. thermal　4. kinetic) energy in the Earth's crust.

(b)　Standard deviation is a mathematical formula that measures the spread of numbers in a data set compared to the (1. absolute
2. minimum　3. maximum　4. average) of those numbers.

(c)　pH is a quantitative (1. tool　2. method　3. measure　4. scale) of the acidity or basicity of aqueous or other liquid solutions.

(d)　The first two digits of this serial number (1. represent　2. replace
3. refine　4. reserve) the country of origin.

(e)　Dragging the zoom slider or clicking the plus or minus button changes the (1. percentage　2. orientation　3. magnification
4. structure) of a worksheet.

(f)　(1. Tree　2. Exploded　3. Cross-section　4. Schematic) diagrams of electrical circuits show how the circuit components are connected together.

(g)　The monitoring system (1. notifies　2. reduces　3. instructs　4. assists) the risk.

(h)　The research (1. emitted　2. presumed　3. resumed　4. installed) after the midpoint evaluation completed.

(i)　We heated and cooled the substance (1. alternately　2. ambiently　3. alchemically　4. aerodynamically) to test its strength under extreme conditions.

(j)　The solar panel is a much cleaner energy source than fossil fuels in (1. because　2. so　3. what　4. that) it does not produce any emissions.

Ⅳ　次の (a) から (d) の各組の英文が同じ意味になるように、（　）に入れるべき最適な語を下の 1 から 10 より選び、その番号を解答欄に記入しなさい。なお、1 から 10 は 1 回しか使えません。文頭に来るべき語であっても先頭は小文字になっています。

(a)　┌　There is really no difference in their mechanical performances, and the only difference is in their designs.

　　　│　(　　　　　) for their designs, there is no difference in their mechanical performances.
　　　└

(b)　┌　A drone is a type of aircraft without any person on board and is controlled by a pilot on the ground.

　　　│　A drone is an (　　　　　) aircraft and controlled by someone on the ground.
　　　└

(c) ⎧ A lunar eclipse occurs when the sun, earth, and moon are in a
　　⎪ straight line.
　　⎨
　　⎪ A lunar eclipse occurs when the sun, earth, and moon are
　　⎩ precisely (　　　　).

(d) ⎧ Pull the power cord of the device out of an outlet before
　　⎪ cleaning or servicing.
　　⎨
　　⎪ (　　　　) the device before cleaning or servicing.
　　⎩

1.　manned　　　2.　empower　　3.　manual　　　4.　except

5.　centered　　6.　aligned　　　7.　unmanned　　8.　apart

9.　accept　　　10. unplug

Ⅴ　次の (a) から (f) の英文がそれぞれ和文と同じ意味になるように、(　)
　に入れるべき最適な語を下の 1 から 15 より選び、その番号を解答欄に
　記入しなさい。なお、1 から 15 は 1 回しか使えません。文頭に来るべ
　き語であっても先頭は小文字になっています。

(a)　Copper and aluminum are used to make electrical wires because
　　 they (　　　　) electricity to flow through them.

　　 銅やアルミニウムは電気よく通すので電線に使用される。

(b)　Greenhouse gases in the earth's atmosphere (　　　　　) as a
　　 blanket to make the earth comfortable.

　　 地球の大気にある温室ガスは毛布のような役割があり、地球を
　　 快適にしている。

21

(c) Under the law, all food manufacturers must inform consumers of the (　　　　) they use in their products.

法律では、全ての食品製造業者は製品にどのような材料を使っ ているかを消費者に公表しなければならない。

(d) (　　　　　) accidents of heavy-duty vehicles carrying hazardous substances are increasing, the state may lower their speed limits.

有害な物質を運ぶトラックの事故が増えているため、州はこれ らの車の制限速度を下げるかもしれない。

(e) (　　　　　) sales figures clearly show that consumers are not buying the product, the company has decided to increase its production volume.

消費者がこの製品を買っていないことが数字で明らかに出てい るにも関わらず、会社はこの製品の新バージョンを発売しよう としている。

(f) (　　　　) of sunlight occurs when white light passing through a prism is separated into its component colors.

プリズムを通過する白色光がその構成要素の色に分離されると きに、日光の分散が起こる。

1. have	2. why	3. ingredients	4. however
5. although	6. gradient	7. dispersion	8. deviating
9. serve	10. warm	11. since	12. allow
13. generate	14. gratitude	15. until	

Ⅵ　次の英文を読んで、各設問に答えなさい。

　　a Water is a vital compound for living things. It is an inorganic compound in the body, (①) up 55% to 60% of the body weight in average adults. b Water works as a solvent to carry nutrients, oxygen and wastes throughout the body. It is also a participant in chemical reactions. It helps ② break down food we eat into smaller molecules. c It allows the body to absorb and release heat slowly when temperature is higher, thereby maintaining a stable body temperature. It serves as a (③) at joints to prevent bones from rubbing together. d

(a) (①) に入る最適な単語を次の 1 から 4 より選び、その番号を解答欄に記入しなさい。

1. make
2. made
3. making
4. makes

(b) 下線部②を言い換える最適な単語を次の 1 から 4 より選び、その番号を解答欄に記入しなさい。

1. consumption
2. digestion
3. dieting
4. respiration

(c)（ ③ ）に入る最適な単語を次の 1 から 4 より選び、その番号を解答欄に記入しなさい。

1. reactant

2. adhesive

3. power

4. lubricant

(d) この英文からは Water has an important role as a thermoregulator. という文章が抜けています。この文章を入れるのに最適な位置を次の 1 から 4 より選び、その番号を解答欄に記入しなさい。

1. [a]
2. [b]
3. [c]
4. [d]

Ⅶ　次の (a) から (f) について、各和文の意味を表すように 1 から 7 を並べか
　　えて英文を作り、3 番目と 5 番目にくる語の番号を解答欄に記入しなさい。

(a) IoT とは、インターネットを介して情報を共有し合う機器を表している。

　　The IoT refers to (1. via　2. information　3. share　4. that
　　5. with　6. one another　7. devices) the Internet.

(b) この警告装置は、後ろから車が近づいてくると自転車の運転者に
　　知らせてくれる。

　　This warning device (1. is　2. let　3. a car　4. will　5. cyclists
　　6. when　7. know) coming up behind them.

(c) その補助金によって、当社は特許取得済の AI 技術の開発を継続で
　　きるだろう。

　　The grant will (1. continue　2. of　3. us　4. the development
　　5. enable　6. our patented　7. to) AI technology.

(d) 太陽から遠く離れた宇宙船は、必要な電力を得るために大きな太
　　陽電池パネルを利用する。

　　Spacecraft (1. from the sun　2. to get　3. traveling　4. large
　　5. use　6. far away　7. solar panels) the electricity they need.

(e) この光学素子を通過したレーザー光は、屈折して一点に収束する。

　　Laser rays that pass through (1. optical　2. this　3. refracted
　　4. device　5. converge　6. and　7. are) at a point.

(f) 鳥は飛べるように体重を最低限に抑えつつ、必要なエネルギーを体
　　内に取り込まなければならない。

　　Birds must provide their bodies with (1. energy　2. weight
　　3. minimizing　4. necessary　5. their　6. while　7. body) to fly.

Ⅰ　次の (a) から (j) の各英語について、最適な日本語を選び、その番号を解答欄に記入しなさい。

(a) comprehensive
- 1. 包括的な
- 2. 部分的な
- 3. 一時的な

(b) inert
- 1. 防湿の
- 2. 不活性の
- 3. 夜行の

(c) coordinates
- 1. 偏差
- 2. 虚数
- 3. 座標

(d) circulation
- 1. 加速
- 2. 分裂
- 3. 循環

(e) deploy
- 1. 配備する
- 2. 巻き込む
- 3. 統合する

(f) intensity
- 1. 許容度
- 2. 強度
- 3. 粘度

(g) surplus
- 1. 余剰
- 2. 規定
- 3. 特徴

(h) modulation
- 1. 伝導
- 2. 変調
- 3. 増幅

(i) supervise
- 1. 監督する
- 2. 具現化する
- 3. 改造する

(j) constellation
- 1. 恒星
- 2. 惑星
- 3. 星座

Ⅱ　次の (a) から (j) の各日本語について、最適な英語を選び、その番号を解答欄に記入しなさい。

(a) 不定の
- 1. provisional
- 2. indefinite
- 3. comparable

(b) 飽和
- 1. adhesion
- 2. dilution
- 3. saturation

(c) 閾 (しきい) 値
- 1. index
- 2. vicinity
- 3. threshold

(d) 分解する
1. disassemble
2. magnify
3. encrypt

(e) 重力の
1. conventional
2. stationary
3. gravitational

(f) 鉱物
1. lava
2. mineral
3. clay

(g) 衝突する
1. incorporate
2. penetrate
3. collide

(h) 放物線
1. parabola
2. gradient
3. hyperbola

(i) 評価する
1. substitute
2. evaluate
3. integrate

(j) 抽出
1. extraction
2. conservation
3. refraction

Ⅲ　次の (a) から (d) の英語の説明に対応する語を下の 1 から 10 より選び、その番号を解答欄に記入しなさい。なお、1 から 10 は 1 回しか使えない。

(a) A mobile computing device that has a flat, rectangular form like that of a magazine or pad of paper

(b) Any unexpected or dangerous effects caused by the administration of a drug in pharmacology

(c) A substance that makes a chemical reaction happen more quickly without itself being changed

(d) An animal or plant that lives on or in an organism of another species to get nutrients

1. acid   2. predator   3. server   4. tablet
5. adverse reaction 6. compound   7. desktop   8. parasite
9. catalyst   10. reverse reaction

Ⅳ　次の (a) から (d) の各組の英文が同じ意味になるよう、（　）に入れる最適な語を下の 1 から 10 より選び、その番号を解答欄に記入しなさい。なお、1 から 10 は 1 回しか使えない。

(a)　Regular maintenance can help to make the life of the equipment longer.

　　Regular maintenance can help to (　　　　) the life of the equipment.

(b)　The mass of an object remains constant without being affected by where it is measured.

　　The mass of an object remains constant (　　　　) of where it is measured.

(c)　Flood hazard maps show areas that are likely to be influenced by flooding during heavy rainfall.

　　Flood hazard maps show areas that are (　　　　) to flooding during heavy rainfall.

(d)　Multiple users with different programs interact with the CPU of a remote server at the same time.

　　Multiple users with different programs interact (　　　　) with the CPU of a remote server.

1. frequently　　2. extend　　3. accessible　　4. susceptible

5. instead　　6. regardless　　7. affected　　8. simultaneously

9. execute　　10. totally

V 次の (a) から (h) の英文を完成させる語として、最適なものをそれぞ
れの1から4より選び、その番号を解答欄に記入しなさい。

(a) (1. Since　2. But　3. Because　4. Although) mechanical watches
are not as accurate as quartz watches, a lot of people buy them.

(b) Each student is (1. copied　2. encoded　3. told　4. infected) to
write a summary of the experiment in English.

(c) The nerve fiber serves (1. to　2. as　3. for　4. at) a relay station
in which each point sends and receives electrical signals.

(d) The report says some elderly people suffer from iron (1. default
2. delay　3. decoy　4. deficiency) in their diet.

(e) Our ultimate goal is to (1. replace　2. remind　3. convert
4. resolve) gasoline with non-polluting energy sources within 10
years.

(f) It will take many years (1. when　2. after　3. before　4. for)
anyone can predict a hurricane's behavior more accurately.

(g) The IC chip contains (1. biochemical　2. biometric　3. antibiotic
4. amphibian) data including an image of the holder's face and
other personal details.

(h) At first (1. manner　2. contact　3. glance　4. breath) this line
looks longer than that one, but it is an optical illusion.

VI 次の英文を読んで、各設問に答えなさい。

If you conduct most of your searches through a non-private search engine, then third-party websites and other unknown entities might track your every move. According to a study of the top one million websites, the web is full of third-party trackers. News websites are some of the worst offenders, with an average of 40 trackers (　①　) in the background. Even if you (　②　) the "do not track" feature of a search engine, those are only voluntary browser requests. ③ <u>A tech giant can analyze your entire online footprint to paint a remarkably accurate picture of you.</u>

(a) 英文に最も合う見出しを次の 1 から 4 より選び、その番号を解答欄に記入しなさい。

1. News websites offend third-party websites and other unknown entities

2. Using a non-private search engine could allow tech companies to track and analyze you

3. The "do not track" feature of a search engine should not be requested voluntarily

4. How the top one million websites know the public and private sides of a user

(b) (　①　) に入る最適な語を次の 1 から 4 より選び、その番号を解答欄に記入しなさい。

1. washing

2. walking

3. seeing

4. running

32

(c) （　②　）に入る最適な語を次の 1 から 4 より選び、その番号を解答欄に記入しなさい。

1. enable

2. stop

3. eliminate

4. convert

(d) 下線部③に最も近い意味の文を次の 1 から 4 より選び、その番号を解答欄に記入しなさい。

1. 巨大な IT 企業ともなると、どのようにインターネットを利用しているのかを驚くくらい正確に知りえることができる。

2. 分析を得意とする巨大な IT 企業は、どれくらいインターネットの利用法が違うかを驚くくらい正確に知っている。

3. 巨大な IT 企業は、ユーザのネット利用の全履歴を分析し、そのユーザを驚くほど正確に知ることができる。

4. 巨大な IT 網をつぶさに分析することによって、ユーザのネット利用の全履歴を非常に正確に割り出すことができる。

Ⅶ　次の (a) から (f) について、各和文の意味を表すように 1 から 7 を並べかえて英文を作り、3 番目と 5 番目にくる語の番号を解答欄に記入しなさい。ただし、文頭に来るべき語であっても（　）内では先頭は小文字になっている。

(a) チームの目標は、顧客がなるべく簡単にこの装置を組み立てられるようにすることだ。

The team's goal is to (1. easier　2. of　3. make　4. the device 5. the assembly　6. their　7. for) customers.

(b) 彗星から放出された塵とガスは、太陽とは反対の方向に伸びる尾を形成する。

The dust and gases spewed from a comet (1. form　2. away 3. stretches　4. from　5. that　6. the sun　7. a tail).

(c) 不要な殺虫剤をお持ちの場合、生き物や環境を保護するために安全に処分してください。

If you have pesticide products not in use, safely (1. living　2. of 3. protect　4. things　5. to　6. the pesticides　7. dispose) and the environment.

(d) モーターの回転が止まったのを確認した後、安全カバーを外してください。

(1. that　2. stopped　3. ensure　4. before　5. the　6. has 7. motor) removing the safety cover.

(e) 環境に配慮した自動車の国内生産は、去年よりも 6 ％増加した。

(1. cars　2. of　3. production　4. a　5. eco-friendly　6. showed 7. domestic) 6% increase over last year.

(f) オゾン層は、太陽から来る有害な紫外線の大部分を吸収してくれる。

The ozone layer absorbs (1. the　2. most　3. harmful　4. ultraviolet 5. coming　6. rays　7. of) from the sun.

第 130 回（2022. 11）

I　次の (a) から (j) の各英語について、最適な日本語を選び、その番号を解答欄に記入しなさい。

(a) assessment
1. 課題
2. 配置
3. 査定

(b) centrifugal
1. らせん状の
2. 遠心の
3. 逆方向の

(c) incline
1. 支点
2. 平衡
3. 斜面

(d) sterilize
1. 滅菌する
2. 蒸溜する
3. 精製する

(e) rubber
1. 膜
2. ゴム
3. 樹脂

(f) dimension
1. 質量
2. 倍率
3. 次元

(g) halt
  1. 休止
  2. 屈折
  3. 診断

(h) adjoin
  1. 復元する
  2. 隣接する
  3. 交換する

(i) requisite
  1. 広範囲の
  2. 代替の
  3. 必須の

(j) tissue
  1. 組織
  2. 動脈
  3. 腫瘍

Ⅱ　次の (a) から (j) の各日本語について、最適な英語を選び、その番号を解答欄に記入しなさい。

(a) 補償
  1. compensation
  2. deficiency
  3. inventory

(b) 任意の
  1. auxiliary
  2. arbitrary
  3. approximately

(c) 揮発性
  1. elasticity
  2. durability
  3. volatility

(d)　振動する
$\left\{\begin{array}{l} 1.\ \text{oscillate} \\ 2.\ \text{insulate} \\ 3.\ \text{withstand} \end{array}\right.$

(e)　減法
$\left\{\begin{array}{l} 1.\ \text{factorization} \\ 2.\ \text{subtraction} \\ 3.\ \text{multiplication} \end{array}\right.$

(f)　対称
$\left\{\begin{array}{l} 1.\ \text{distortion} \\ 2.\ \text{lattice} \\ 3.\ \text{symmetry} \end{array}\right.$

(g)　自発的に
$\left\{\begin{array}{l} 1.\ \text{substantially} \\ 2.\ \text{spontaneously} \\ 3.\ \text{thoroughly} \end{array}\right.$

(h)　障害物
$\left\{\begin{array}{l} 1.\ \text{obstacle} \\ 2.\ \text{defective} \\ 3.\ \text{facility} \end{array}\right.$

(i)　断片化
$\left\{\begin{array}{l} 1.\ \text{assimilation} \\ 2.\ \text{galvanization} \\ 3.\ \text{fragmentation} \end{array}\right.$

(j)　除去する
$\left\{\begin{array}{l} 1.\ \text{transcribe} \\ 2.\ \text{eliminate} \\ 3.\ \text{identify} \end{array}\right.$

Ⅲ　次の (a) から (d) の英語の説明に対応する語を下の 1 から 10 より選び、その番号を解答欄に記入しなさい。なお、 1 から 10 は 1 回しか使えない。

(a) An application software to access the Internet and retrieve the necessary content

(b) A sudden rise in the incidence of a disease such as pneumonia, measles, or Covid-19

(c) Having no net addition of carbon dioxide to the atmosphere

(d) The process of determining the most important people or things from among a large number that require attention

1. peak　　　　2. spreadsheet　3. classification　4. database

5. carbonization 6. browser　　　7. arrangement　8. carbon-neutral

9. triage　　　10. outbreak

Ⅳ　次の (a) から (d) の各組の英文が同じ意味になるよう、（　）に入れる
　　最適な語を下の 1 から 10 より選び、その番号を解答欄に記入しなさい。
　　なお、1 から 10 は 1 回しか使えない。

(a)　You can apply for the technical training courses through the
　　 Internet or by phone.

　　 You can apply for the technical training courses (　　　　)
　　 or by phone.

(b)　The adhesive strength of the new tape is five times as high as
　　 that of the standard tape.

　　 The new tape (　　　　　) five times the adhesive strength of
　　 the standard tape.

(c)　The battery can be used for up to 90 minutes after it is fully
　　 charged.

　　 The battery (　　　　) 90 minutes after it is fully charged.

(d)　At 1 atm pressure, gold changes its phase from solid to liquid at
　　 about 1063°C.

　　 At 1 atm pressure, gold (　　　　) at about 1063°C.

1.	does	2.	uses	3.	has	4.	online
5.	lasts	6.	digital	7.	melts	8.	is
9.	evaporates	10.	accumulates				

V 次の (a) から (h) の英文を完成させる語として、最適なものをそれぞれの 1 から 4 より選び、その番号を解答欄に記入しなさい。

(a) When the (1. infrared　2. investment　3. visibility　4. automation) is low, pilots have to rely more on the plane's instruments for navigation.

(b) These two devices are (1. sort　2. resemble　3. kindly　4. alike) in appearance, but not in how they work.

(c) The annual share of renewable energy power generation in Europe has already (1. eliminated　2. expected　3. estimated 4. exceeded) 40%.

(d) The gravitational force that the moon (1. exerts　2. sends 3. affects　4. pushes) on the earth causes tides to rise and fall.

(e) Astronomers believe (1. which　2. that　3. what　4. the fact that) we can see through telescopes makes up less than 5% of the mass of the universe.

(f) Climate change can be defined as a (1. pacific　2. permanent 3. peripheral　4. punctual) change in weather conditions.

(g) (1. Reserving　2. Ratifying　3. Rotating　4. Recycling) the tires of a car every few months helps them last longer.

(h) A ship receives radio signals (1. transmits　2. to transmit 3. transmitting　4. transmitted) from GPS satellites to determine its position.

Ⅵ 次の英文を読んで、各設問に答えなさい。

Capsaicin is a chemical compound that gives peppers their spicy taste and has many beneficial effects. Since tomatoes are closely (①) to peppers, they have all the genes necessary to produce capsaicinoids; however, these genes are not active in tomatoes. Scientists hope to activate these genes through genetic engineering because capsaicin contained in peppers has been shown to have anti-inflammatory, anti-oxidant, and weight-loss properties. ② <u>Peppers grown outdoors are susceptible to harsh weather and vulnerable to soil-borne diseases</u> whereas tomatoes are often grown indoors and much easier to cultivate. Scientists hope that tomatoes will produce capsaicinoids at a commercial level in the future.

(a) 英文に最も合う見出しを、次の1から4より選び、その番号を解答欄に記入しなさい。

1. The Reason Scientists Want to Engineer Tomatoes
2. Genes to Produce Capsaicinoids
3. How to Create Better-Tasting Tomatoes
4. Beneficial Effects of Capsaicin

(b) (①) に入る最適な語を次の1から4より選び、その番号を解答欄に記入しなさい。

1. relative
2. relation
3. relationship
4. related

(c) 下線部②に最も近い意味の文を次の 1 から 4 より選び、その番号を解答欄に記入しなさい。

1. 屋外で成長した胡椒は、悪天候に強いが、土壌にいる外敵に弱い。

2. 屋外で作られた胡椒は、厳しい天候に影響されやすいが、土壌による病気には強い。

3. 屋外で作られる胡椒は、厳しい天候に影響されやすく、土壌に起因する病気に弱い。

4. 屋外で成長する胡椒は、天候の変化には影響されないが、土壌に起因する病気には弱い。

(d) 英文の内容と一致しないものを次の 1 から 4 より選び、その番号を解答欄に記入しなさい。

1. Capsaicin is a pure element.
2. Peppers have properties good for your health.
3. Tomatoes are easier to grow.
4. Scientists have not succeeded in producing capsaicin derived from tomatoes at a commercial level.

Ⅶ　次の (a) から (f) について、各和文の意味を表すように１から７を並べかえて英文を作り、３番目と５番目にくる語の番号を解答欄に記入しなさい。ただし、文頭に来るべき語であっても（　　）内では先頭は小文字になっている。

(a) 人体には多くの神経終末があり、接触に反応する。

Our bodies have a lot (1. respond　2. touch　3. which　4. nerve 5. to　6. endings　7. of).

(b) 航空機は、長期間使用されていないときは、ジェットエンジンの吸気口に覆いがされる。

The air (1. covered　2. engine　3. a　4. is　5. of　6. intake　7. jet) when a plane is not used for a long period.

(c) 黒点は、太陽の他のどの場所よりも磁場が強い領域である。

Sunspots are areas (1. the magnetic　2. stronger　3. where　4.is 5. anywhere　6. than　7. field) else on the sun.

(d) コンピュータの周辺機器としては、入出力装置や記憶装置などが挙げられる。

(1. includes　2. of　3. I/O devices　4. peripheral　5. computer 6. equipment　7. a) and storage.

(e) 詳しく調査すれば、肉眼では見えない損傷がはっきりする。

A further investigation will reveal damage (1. invisible　2. the　3. that 4. naked　5. to　6. eye　7. is).

(f) 効果的な対策を講じるために真因を突き止めることが必要である。

It is necessary to (1. the　2. to　3. cause　4. root　5. out 6. develop　7. find) an effective countermeasure.

第 129 回（2022. 6）

I　次の (a) から (j) の各英語について、最適な日本語を選び、その番号を解答欄に記入しなさい。

(a) ductile
  1. 無機の
  2. 可燃性の
  3. 延性の

(b) encryption
  1. 合理化
  2. 暗号化
  3. 多様化

(c) braking
  1. 衝撃
  2. 破損
  3. 制動

(d) ellipse
  1. 楕円
  2. 双曲線
  3. 円錐

(e) intermedium
  1. 副産物
  2. 媒介物
  3. 異物

(f) feasibility
  1. 重要性
  2. 完全性
  3. 可能性

(g)　precede
1. 先行する
2. 予測する
3. 保持する

(h)　longitudinal
1. 良性の
2. 空中の
3. 縦の

(i)　prediction
1. 予測
2. 蓄積
3. 共振

(j)　sustain
1. 持続させる
2. 密閉する
3. 偏光させる

Ⅱ　次の (a) から (j) の各日本語について、最適な英語を選び、その番号を解答欄に記入しなさい。

(a)　定格の
1. extensive
2. infinite
3. rated

(b)　ナトリウム
1. chlorine
2. sodium
3. iodine

(c)　矛盾
1. contradiction
2. distinction
3. interaction

(d) 消化する $\left\{\begin{array}{l}\text{1. voyage} \\ \text{2. exhibit} \\ \text{3. digest}\end{array}\right.$

(e) 変数 $\left\{\begin{array}{l}\text{1. innumerable} \\ \text{2. variable} \\ \text{3. expendable}\end{array}\right.$

(f) 内部 $\left\{\begin{array}{l}\text{1. interior} \\ \text{2. interface} \\ \text{3. insulation}\end{array}\right.$

(g) 不透明な $\left\{\begin{array}{l}\text{1. turbulent} \\ \text{2. primitive} \\ \text{3. opaque}\end{array}\right.$

(h) 回収する $\left\{\begin{array}{l}\text{1. repel} \\ \text{2. retrieve} \\ \text{3. resume}\end{array}\right.$

(i) 妥当性 $\left\{\begin{array}{l}\text{1. validity} \\ \text{2. performance} \\ \text{3. allotment}\end{array}\right.$

(j) 速度 $\left\{\begin{array}{l}\text{1. oscillation} \\ \text{2. velocity} \\ \text{3. coefficient}\end{array}\right.$

Ⅲ　次の (a) から (d) の英語の説明に対応する語を下の 1 から 10 より選び、その番号を解答欄に記入しなさい。なお、 1 から 10 は 1 回しか使えない。

(a) The result you get by adding two or more amounts together and dividing the total by the number of amounts

(b) A device that directly converts the energy of light into electrical energy through the photovoltaic effect*

(c) Our immune system is trained to create antibodies, just as it does when it's exposed to a disease

(d) The point on a triangle that is opposite to the base of the triangle

［注］photovoltaic effect* : 光起電効果

1.　fuel cell　　2.　medicine　　3.　angle　　　4.　solar cell

5.　multiple　　6.　toe　　　　7.　injection　　8.　average

9.　apex　　　　10. vaccine

Ⅳ 次の (a) から (d) の各組の英文が同じ意味になるよう、（ ）に入れる
最適な語を下の 1 から 10 より選び、その番号を解答欄に記入しなさい。
なお、1 から 10 は 1 回しか使えない。

(a) Excessive exhaust smoke may indicate that the engine needs a
thorough examination and repair.

Excessive exhaust smoke may indicate that the engine
needs an (   ).

(b) Sun, wind, and rivers are increasingly taking the place of fossil
fuels as sources of energy.

Sun, wind, and rivers are increasingly (   ) fossil fuels
as sources of energy.

(c) CDC is the abbreviation of Centers for Disease Control and
Prevention, the national public health agency of the United States.

CDC (   ) for Centers for Disease Control and Prevention,
the national public health agency of the United States.

(d) Copper allows heat to pass through it faster than glass.

Copper has higher thermal (   ) than glass.

1. temperature　2. implies　　3. represents　4. overcoming

5. resistance　　6. overhaul　　7. alignment　　8. conductivity

9. replacing　　10. stands

Ⅴ　次の (a) から (h) の英文を完成させる語として、最適なものをそれぞれの1から4より選び、その番号を解答欄に記入しなさい。

(a) (1. Even　2. What　3. When　4. Then) if a device is not sending or receiving data, it still uses bandwidth.

(b) Several (1. things　2. one　3. hard　4. pieces) of equipment were provided for the study, but none of them was used.

(c) The statistics (1. tell　2. say　3. whisper　4. call) us that surfing the internet is the most popular activity after 8 p.m.

(d) The share of renewable energy in total electricity generation in the country has increased (1. at　2. by　3. for　4. between) 8%.

(e) (1. Away from　2. Except for　3. Unlike　4. Instead of) MERS and SARS, Covid-19 can be transmitted by people who are mildly ill or show no symptoms.

(f) Using chemicals or other hazardous substances can put your health at (1. risk　2. will　3. rest　4. odds).

(g) A pathogen is any organism that can (1. cure　2. strengthen　3. arise　4. cause) disease in a person, animal, or plant.

(h) Contrary to our expectations, no significant differences were (1. interrupted　2. observed　3. achieved　4. forecast) between the telephone and the face-to-face surveys.

Ⅵ　次の英文を読んで、各設問に答えなさい。

A meteor shower occurs when the earth passes through a field of debris* on its orbit around the sun. ① <u>When the earth plows through such a stream of debris, space rocks tumble into the atmosphere.</u> The rocks (②) as air drag heats up and ignites them. Most meteors completely burn up in the atmosphere. The rare rock that hits the ground is called a meteorite. The shower starts slowly, as our planet enters the debris field, and (③) when Earth passes through the most crowded part of the field, and again trails off as we leave.

［注］a field of debris* : 岩石群

(a) 英文に最も合う見出しを次の 1 から 4 より選び、その番号を解答欄に記入しなさい。

1.　Why Meteor Showers Occur

2.　Meteor Shower as the Most Crowded Part of Debris

3.　The Collision of the Earth and a Meteorite

4.　Air Drag Heats Up and Ignites Debris

(b) 下線部①に最も近い意味の文を次の 1 から 4 より選び、その番号を解答欄に記入しなさい。

1.　地球がこのような岩石の軌道を通るとき、隕石が大気中に入ってくる。

2.　地球がこのような岩石群のなかを通過するとき、宇宙岩が大気中に入ってくる。

3.　地球と岩石群の軌道が一致するとき、宇宙岩が大気圏内に侵入する。

4.　地球がこのような岩石群のなかを通過するときに宇宙岩が大気によって熱を帯びる。

(c)（　②　）に入る最適な語を次の 1 から 4 より選び、その番号を解答欄に記入しなさい。

1. slow
2. glow
3. blow
4. flow

(d)（　③　）に入る最適な語を次の 1 から 4 より選び、その番号を解答欄に記入しなさい。

1. comes
2. exits
3. stops
4. peaks

Ⅶ 次の (a) から (f) について、各和文の意味を表すように 1 から 7 を並べかえて英文を作り、3 番目と 5 番目にくる語の番号を解答欄に記入しなさい。ただし、文頭に来るべき語であっても（　）内では先頭は小文字になっている。

(a) 近い将来、自律運転するクルマを利用できるようになるだろう。

It is said (1. will　2. autonomous　3. fully　4. be　5. cars 6. available　7. that) in the near future.

(b) 雪は、気温が氷点下のときに雲で発生する氷晶の形で空から落ちてきたものである。

Snow is precipitation in the form of ice crystals (1. temperatures 2. originate　3. that　4. in　5. are　6. when　7. clouds) below the freezing point.

(c) 種子の発芽とは種子が新たな植物となる過程のことである。

Seed germination is the process (1. develop　2. plants　3. new 4. which　5. into　6. seeds　7. through).

(d) 手を洗い、マスクをすることである程度人から人への感染を防ぐことができる。

By washing hands and wearing masks, infections (1. from　2. be 3. spreading　4. to　5. prevented　6. can　7. others) to some extent.

(e) この角パイプはアルミニウム製で、断面が 25mm × 50mm である。

This square pipe (1. of　2. a　3. aluminum　4. cross-section 5. made　6. is　7. with) of 25 mm by 50 mm.

(f) 液体窒素は超低温なため、皮膚損傷の原因となることがある。

(1. cause　2. because　3. injury　4. nitrogen　5. liquid　6. skin 7. may) its temperature is extremely low.

第 128 回 (2022.1)

I　次の (a) から (j) の各英語について、最適な日本語を選び、その番号を解答欄に記入しなさい。

(a) lapse
1. 誘導
2. 経過
3. 粘着

(b) deviation
1. 比重
2. 偏差
3. 変調

(c) conventional
1. 従来の
2. 無限の
3. 回転の

(d) facilitate
1. 容易にする
2. 操縦する
3. 改訂する

(e) synthesis
1. 合成
2. 刺激
3. 制動

(f) substantial
1. 不可逆の
2. 実質の
3. 循環性の

(g) precision
1. 露光
2. 識別
3. 精密

(h) yield
1. 積載
2. 配列
3. 生産高

(i) decoder
1. 中継機
2. 復号器
3. 平衡装置

(j) enrich
1. 濃厚にする
2. 柔軟にする
3. 創造する

Ⅱ　次の (a) から (j) の各日本語について、最適な英語を選び、その番号を解答欄に記入しなさい。

(a) 振動
1. conduction
2. oscillation
3. acceleration

(b) 原稿
1. brochure
2. manuscript
3. publication

(c) 貫通する
1. restructure
2. violate
3. penetrate

(d)　石油
{
1. petroleum
2. kerosene
3. catalyst

(e)　わずかに
{
1. thoroughly
2. slightly
3. instantly

(f)　補助の
{
1. auxiliary
2. respective
3. inherited

(g)　免疫
{
1. microbe
2. chromosome
3. immunity

(h)　陽極*
＊P.154-155 をご確認ください。
{
1. cathode
2. armature
3. anode

(i)　現れる
{
1. rationalize
2. appear
3. immerse

(j)　目的
{
1. objective
2. query
3. gain

Ⅲ 次の (a) から (d) の英語の説明に対応する語を下の 1 から 10 より選び、その番号を解答欄に記入しなさい。なお、1 から 10 は 1 回しか使えない。

(a) A protein produced in the blood that fights diseases by attacking and killing harmful bacteria and viruses

(b) An extremely large group of stars and planets that make up the universe

(c) The process of gradual change that happens to plants and animals over time

(d) A substance such as oil that is put on surfaces, especially parts of a machine, in order to make them move smoothly

1. galaxy　　　　2. friction　　　3. evolution　4. antibody

5. lubricant　　　6. pathogen　　7. gasoline　8. black hole

9. transformation　10. cluster

Ⅳ　次の (a) から (d) の各組の英文が同じ意味になるよう、（　）に入れる最適な語を下の 1 から 10 より選び、その番号を解答欄に記入しなさい。なお、1 から 10 は 1 回しか使えない。文頭に来るべき語であっても先頭は小文字になっている。

(a)　Free from the influence of daily sunlight, mimosa* leaves continue to follow their normal daily cycle.
　　　［注］mimosa* : ミモザ（植物）

　　　(　　　　) of daily sunlight, mimosa leaves continue to follow their normal daily cycle.

(b)　The chemist determined that the substance was sodium through an experiment.

　　　The chemist (　　　　) the substance as sodium through an experiment.

(c)　If you smoke heavily for years, you may lose your health.

　　　Heavy smoking for years may adversely (　　　) your health.

(d)　The number of machines in the factory is more than necessary.

　　　The factory has some (　　　) machines.

1.　identified　　2.　redundant　　3.　effect　　4.　despite

5.　improved　　6.　affect　　7.　independent　8.　installed

9.　important　　10. separate

V　次の (a) から (h) の英文を完成させる語として、最適なものをそれぞ
れの 1 から 4 より選び、その番号を解答欄に記入しなさい。

(a)　Modern airplanes are lighter and have better (1. dynasty
2. duplicate　3. aerodynamics　4. physics), so they consume less
fuel.

(b)　This software is very useful (1. totally　2. although　3. somewhat
4. because) it automatically corrects any calculation mistakes.

(c)　The cracks on the road are all caused by the (1. intense　2. over
3. large　4. inserting) heat during the summer.

(d)　A photovoltaic (PV) cell, known as a solar cell, is a device that
(1. produces　2. transmits　3. Exchanges　4. converts) sunlight
directly into electricity.

(e)　TV remote controllers have a small light-emitting diode, from
which infrared (1. mirror　2. radiation　3. lamp　4. evolution)
comes out.

(f)　Decomposers play a vital role in the ecosystem by (1. composing
2. destroying　3. returning　4. taking) organic matter to soil.

(g)　A large amount of plastic waste flowing into the oceans has
(1. negative　2. individual　3. fragile　4. few) impacts on marine
creatures.

(h)　Weather satellites (1. rescue　2. rotate　3. broadcast　4. observe)
the earth by taking pictures from the same location at regular
intervals.

Ⅵ 次の英文を読んで、各設問に答えなさい。

① NASA's quest to understand how the universe works starts with the study of the basic building blocks of our existence—matter, energy, space, and time—and how they behave under the extreme physical conditions that characterize the infant and evolving universe. The Physics of the Cosmos (PCOS) program includes cosmology, high-energy astrophysics, and fundamental physics projects aimed at ② addressing central questions about the nature of complex astrophysical phenomena such as black holes, neutron stars, dark energy, and (③) waves. By utilizing a variety of space-based missions, PCOS's final, overall goal is to learn about the origin and ultimate destiny of the cosmos.

(a) 英文に最も合う見出しを、次の1から4より選び、その番号を解答欄に記入しなさい。

1. Study of the Basic Building Blocks of Our Existence

2. Goal of the PCOS Program

3. Space-based Missions

4. Origin and Goal of the Cosmos

(b) 下線部①に最も近い意味の文を次の1から4より選び、その番号を解答欄に記入しなさい。

1. NASAが宇宙の働きを探求する際は、宇宙の構成要素の問題やエネルギー源、場所や時間について研究することから始めます。

2. NASAが宇宙の働きを探求する際は、私たちの存在が何をもとに作られているか、その内容やエネルギー源、いつどこで始まったかを研究の基礎とします。

3. 宇宙の仕組みを理解しようとする NASA の探求は、私たちの存在の基本的な構成要素である物質、エネルギー、空間、時間について研究することから始まります。

4. 宇宙の仕組みを理解しようとする NASA の探求は、基礎的構造を私たちの存在問題として取り組み、物質、エネルギー、場所や時間について研究することから始めます。

(c) 下線部②に最も近い意味を次の 1 から 4 より選び、その番号を解答欄に記入しなさい。

1. sending with
2. serving with
3. dealing with
4. cooperating with

(d) （　③　）に入る最も適切な語を次の 1 から 4 より選び、その番号を解答欄に記入しなさい。

1. acoustic
2. seismic
3. gravitational
4. inertia

Ⅶ　次の (a) から (f) について、各和文の意味を表すように 1 から 7 を並べかえて英文を作り、3 番目と 5 番目にくる語の番号を解答欄に記入しなさい。

(a) 空気圧が高すぎるとコンピュータが判断した場合、全てのエアバルブが開く。

All (1. computer　2. when　3. air valves　4. open　5. that 6. detects　7. the) the air pressure is too high.

(b) 脳がどのように機能するか、なぜ自己認識ができるのかはまだ解明されていない。

We still do not know how (1. have　2. we　3. the　4. and　5. brain 6. why　7. works) a sense of self-awareness.

(c) その後の調査で、原油はパイプラインに生じた小さな亀裂から流出したことが分かった。

The subsequent (1. that　2. had been　3. from　4. revealed 5. discharged　6. investigation　7. the crude oil) a small crack in a pipeline.

(d) 物体の重さは測定する場所によって変わる。

The weight of (1. on　2. an object　3. where　4. is　5. varies　6. it 7. depending) measured.

(e) 生産コスト削減のため、土地が安いところに工場を移設した。

To reduce the production cost, the company (1. the land　2. places 3. its　4. where　5. relocated　6. to　7. factories) was inexpensive.

(f) 優秀な設計者は、CADを使用する能力と同様に、優れた製図技能を有するべきだ。

A competent designer (1. should　2. drawing　3. well　4. as 5. good　6. skills　7. have) as the ability to use CAD.

第 127 回 (2021. 11)

I　次の (a) から (j) の各英語について、最適な日本語を選び、その番号を解答欄に記入しなさい。

(a) conservation
- 1. 保守
- 2. 優先
- 3. 保存

(b) inertia
- 1. 慣性
- 2. 欠点
- 3. 繊維

(c) elimination
- 1. 抽出
- 2. 除去
- 3. 感染

(d) lateral
- 1. 局所的な
- 2. 横方向の
- 3. 周辺の

(e) inversely
- 1. 逆に
- 2. 自然に
- 3. 完全に

(f) fraction
- 1. 格子
- 2. 勾配
- 3. 分数

(g)　substitute
- 1. 代用する
- 2. 軽視する
- 3. 再生する

(h)　shipment
- 1. 交換
- 2. 出荷
- 3. 査定

(i)　isolate
- 1. 分離する
- 2. 変換する
- 3. 維持する

(j)　insulation
- 1. 絶縁
- 2. 配置
- 3. 認識

Ⅱ　次の (a) から (j) の各日本語について、最適な英語を選び、その番号を解答欄に記入しなさい。

(a)　流体
- 1. timber
- 2. layer
- 3. fluid

(b)　重要性
- 1. tolerance
- 2. instance
- 3. significance

(c)　交互に
- 1. regularly
- 2. alternately
- 3. vertically

(d)　係数
$\begin{cases} 1.\ \text{coefficient} \\ 2.\ \text{remainder} \\ 3.\ \text{approximation} \end{cases}$

(e)　溶岩
$\begin{cases} 1.\ \text{germ} \\ 2.\ \text{clay} \\ 3.\ \text{lava} \end{cases}$

(f)　種々雑多の
$\begin{cases} 1.\ \text{microcosmic} \\ 2.\ \text{provisional} \\ 3.\ \text{miscellaneous} \end{cases}$

(g)　耐久力
$\begin{cases} 1.\ \text{durability} \\ 2.\ \text{feasibility} \\ 3.\ \text{probability} \end{cases}$

(h)　弾力性
$\begin{cases} 1.\ \text{analogy} \\ 2.\ \text{elasticity} \\ 3.\ \text{surplus} \end{cases}$

(i)　再開する
$\begin{cases} 1.\ \text{negotiate} \\ 2.\ \text{embody} \\ 3.\ \text{resume} \end{cases}$

(j)　影響を
受けやすい
$\begin{cases} 1.\ \text{intentional} \\ 2.\ \text{susceptible} \\ 3.\ \text{affectional} \end{cases}$

Ⅲ　次の (a) から (d) の英語の説明に対応する語を下の 1 から 10 より選び、その番号を解答欄に記入しなさい。なお、1 から 10 は 1 回しか使えない。

(a) A living thing such as an animal or plant that is capable of reproduction, growth, and maintenance

(b) A round object that turns and rolls over, which allows a vehicle to move along the ground

(c) A software program used to navigate the World Wide Web on the internet

(d) A thin tube which carries blood to your heart from other parts of your body

1.　engine 　　 2.　vent 　　　 3.　mineral 　　 4.　compound

5.　wheel 　　　 6.　display 　　 7.　organism 　　 8.　vessel

9.　browser 　　 10. phenomenon

Ⅳ　次の (a) から (d) の各組の英文が同じ意味になるよう、（ ）に入れる
最適な語を下の 1 から 10 より選び、その番号を解答欄に記入しなさい。
なお、1 から 10 は 1 回しか使えない。

(a)　Concrete block walls are not structurally very strong; therefore,
steel bars are often used to make them stronger.

Concrete block walls are not structurally very strong;
therefore, steel bars are often used to (　　　) them.

(b)　Carbon fibers can be defined as fibers that have a carbon
content of 90% or above.

Carbon fibers can be defined as fibers (　　　) a carbon
content of 90% or above.

(c)　The researchers of the team investigate where life on the earth
came from.

The researchers of the team investigate the (　　　) of life on
the earth.

(d)　According to the survey, the reason for the performance
degradation is an airflow reduction.

The survey has revealed that an airflow reduction (　　　) the
performance degradation.

1.　withstand　　2.　origin　　3.　identifies　　4.　assumes

5.　end　　6.　by　　7.　causes　　8.　with

9.　possibility　　10. reinforce

V 次の (a) から (h) の英文を完成させる語として、最適なものをそれぞ
　　れの 1 から 4 より選び、その番号を解答欄に記入しなさい。

(a) This new device is half the size of the (1. previous　2. pretend
　　3. precious　4. prevailing) model, yet it is twice as powerful.

(b) Before changing the theme of your thesis, you should (1. fail
　　2. condense　3. circulate　4. consult) your supervisor first.

(c) Cosmic rays can be very harmful to humans, so spacesuits should
　　be designed to (1. repel　2. recount　3. resound　4. renovate)
　　them.

(d) The performance of the maglev prototype (1. excess　2. extracted
　　3. exceeded　4. exported) the expectations of the press.

(e) This species of plant is in danger of (1. expansion　2. extinction
　　3. exploration　4. examination).

(f) A dictionary (1. judges　2. decides　3. specify　4. defines) a
　　pandemic as a disease that affects many people over a very wide
　　area.

(g) Household (1. appliances　2. tools　3. instruments　4. lighting)
　　such as heat lamps and toasters use IR radiation to transmit heat.

(h) Unfortunately, it is extremely difficult to (1. predict　2. extend
　　3. imitate　4. launch) earthquakes, especially early enough
　　before they happen.

Ⅵ　次の英文を読んで、各設問に答えなさい。

Encryption is the process of converting data into a cipher text or random data which is meaningless. Here, cipher text means (①) data, which cannot be easily understood by anyone except ② authorized parties. Encryption is done to protect the confidentiality of digital data that is either stored on the computer or is transferred across the network. Decryption is the reverse of encryption. Until decrypted, the cipher text appears as meaningless. ③ To protect data from being decrypted by just anybody on the network, only those users who have the decryption key can decrypt the data and make it useful.

(a) 英文に最も合う見出しを、次の 1 から 4 より選び、その番号を解答欄に記入しなさい。

1.　Disadvantages of Encryption and Decryption
2.　Way of Safely Exchanging Data on Networks
3.　How to Reverse Cipher Text
4.　Attacker Reveals Confidential Data

(b) (①) に入る最適な語を次の 1 から 4 より選び、その番号を解答欄に記入しなさい。

1.　scrambled
2.　decrypted
3.　confidential
4.　meaningless

(c) ②の指す内容として不適切であるものを次の１から４より選び、その番号を解答欄に記入しなさい。

1. users authorized to read the data

2. intended receivers of the data

3. users having the decryption key

4. persons with access to the network

(d) 下線部③に最も近い意味の文を次の１から４より選び、その番号を解答欄に記入しなさい。

1. 暗号化されたデータをネットワーク上の誰もが安全に扱えるよう、復号鍵を持つユーザーのみがデータを復号できる。

2. 暗号化されたデータをネットワーク上の特定の人が安全に扱えるよう、暗号鍵をもつユーザーのみがデータを利用できる。

3. ネットワーク上の特定の人がデータを復号することのないよう、暗号鍵と復号鍵を持つユーザーのみがデータを復号でき利用できる。

4. ネットワーク上の誰もがデータを復号することのないよう、復号鍵を持つユーザーのみがデータを復号でき有用な形にできる。

Ⅶ 次の (a) から (f) について、各和文の意味を表すように１から７を並べかえて英文を作り、３番目と５番目にくる語の番号を解答欄に記入しなさい。

(a) この国の排ガス規制は他の国より厳しい。

This country's (1. stricter　2. those　3. of　4. than　5. are 6. regulations　7. emission) other countries.

(b) 組み立ての際、この 2 つのパーツの間にすき間を作るようにして
ください。

Be sure (1. gap　2. a　3. these　4. to　5. between　6. leave
7. small) two parts during the assembly.

(c) 今日、技術のおかげで世界中の人々とのコミュニケーションが容
易になった。

Today, technology (1. to　2. with　3. made　4. has　5. it
6. communicate　7. easier) other people around the world.

(d) 普通の人であっても宇宙旅行を楽しめる日がもうすぐやって来る。

The day will soon (1. even　2. enjoy　3. come　4. ordinary
5. when　6. can　7. people) traveling in space.

(e) 動物実験なしに開発された化粧品を選んで買う消費者が増えて
いる。

More and more consumers choose to buy (1. developed　2. cosmetics
3. been　4. animal　5. have　6. without　7. that) testing.

(f) x の値を求めるには、方程式の両辺に 2 をかけてください。

Multiply (1. of　2. the　3. two　4. both　5. equation　6. sides
7. by) to find the value of x.

第 126 回（2021. 6）

Ⅰ　次の（a）から（j）の各英語について、最適な日本語を選び、その番号を解答欄に記入しなさい。

(a) lapse
1. 掲示
2. 経過
3. 飽和

(b) convection
1. 反響
2. 放射
3. 対流

(c) decimal point
1. 接点
2. 小数点
3. 特異点

(d) enrich
1. 偏光させる
2. 昇華する
3. 濃縮する

(e) dimension
1. 次元
2. 水準
3. 倍率

(f) hazardous
1. 重大な
2. 危険な
3. 誘導性の

(g) inclination
- 1. 傾斜
- 2. 平衡
- 3. 界面

(h) goods
- 1. 資産
- 2. 商品
- 3. 薬物

(i) clay
- 1. 蒸気
- 2. 栄養素
- 3. 粘土

(j) schematic diagram
- 1. 透視図
- 2. 概略図
- 3. 平面図

Ⅱ　次の (a) から (j) の各日本語について、最適な英語を選び、その番号を解答欄に記入しなさい。

(a) 対称
- 1. coordinates
- 2. proportion
- 3. symmetry

(b) 信頼性
- 1. availability
- 2. reliability
- 3. confidentiality

(c) 逆の
- 1. optimal
- 2. relevant
- 3. inverse

(d) 屈折
- 1. refraction
- 2. contraction
- 3. destruction

(e) 石油
- 1. lubrication
- 2. petroleum
- 3. fuel

(f) 湾
- 1. lava
- 2. gulf
- 3. swamp

(g) 厳密に
- 1. slightly
- 2. obviously
- 3. strictly

(h) 飽和する
- 1. saturate
- 2. manipulate
- 3. resolve

(i) 制動
- 1. braking
- 2. initialization
- 3. resonance

(j) 太陽電池
- 1. dry battery
- 2. hydrogen battery
- 3. solar cell

Ⅲ　次の (a) から (d) の英語の説明に対応する語を下の 1 から 10 より選び、その番号を解答欄に記入しなさい。なお、1 から 10 は 1 回しか使えない。

(a) A small piece of metal or other substance that is used to take an electric current to or from a source of power

(b) A vent in the earth's crust through which molten rock, rock fragments, gases, ashes, and the like are ejected

(c) A short, solid piece of metal that moves up and down inside a cylinder in an engine

(d) The part of mathematics that involves numbers and their addition, subtraction, multiplication, and division

1.　cliff	2.　lift	3.　piston	4.　volcano
5.　arithmetic	6.　shaft	7.　electrode	8.　crack
9.　geometric	10. magnet		

Ⅳ　次の (a) から (d) の各組の英文が同じ意味になるよう、(　) に入れる
　　最適な語を下の 1 から 10 より選び、その番号を解答欄に記入しなさい。
　　なお、1 から 10 は 1 回しか使えない。

(a)　Our proposed system does not require performing much
　　　maintenance during its lifetime.

　　　Our proposed system requires (　　　　　) maintenance
　　　during its lifetime.

(b)　The new medicine shows signs of being successful in curing the
　　　deadly disease.

　　　The new medicine is (　　　　　) as a cure for the deadly
　　　disease.

(c)　The organic compound is made of only hydrogen and carbon
　　　atoms.

　　　The organic compound is a (　　　　　).

(d)　Magnets do not attract material that does not allow electricity
　　　to pass through it under normal conditions.

　　　Magnets do not attract electrically (　　　　　) material under
　　　normal conditions.

1.　activated　　2.　hydrocarbon　3.　little　　4.　carbohydrate
5.　promising　　6.　optical　　　7.　insulating　8.　processing
9.　conducting　 10. few

V 次の (a) から (h) の英文を完成させる語として、最適なものをそれぞ
　　れの 1 から 4 より選び、その番号を解答欄に記入しなさい。

(a) These (1. particles　2. problems　3. purposes　4. agencies) are
so small that we have to use the latest microscope to observe
them.

(b) Welding is a technique used for joining metallic parts usually by
applying (1. medicated　2. heated　3. medication　4. heat).

(c) Animals such as bats can use ultrasound to (1. use　2. hear
3. detect　4. emit) objects and navigate their way through the
darkness.

(d) One of the main causes of foot pain is wearing shoes that do not
fit (1. hard　2. tightly　3. soft　4. properly).

(e) You have to find the right (1. percentage　2. balance　3. load
4. average) between enough workout and enough sleep.

(f) When the heart pumps blood, the blood (1. treats　2. sends
3. acts　4. circulates) around the body through blood vessels.

(g) In Kenya, as (1. much　2. little　3. good　4. bad) as 90% of the
rainforest has disappeared together with the animals living there.

(h) Simultaneous equations are a set of equations with the same
(1. variables　2. numbers　3. questions　4. constants) to be
solved together.

Ⅵ 次の英文を読んで、各設問に答えなさい。

For decades, scientists have dreamed of plastics that can heal themselves like human skin. In 2001, researchers developed a polymer with microscopic capsules containing a liquid healing agent. When the material cracked, the chemicals were released to fill the gaps. ① <u>Then in 2014, engineers inspired by the human blood clotting system created a plastic that can automatically fill wider holes</u>. They designed a network of channels ② <u>resembling</u> blood vessels in the human body so that a healing agent can be delivered to the damaged area, allowing the gap to be sealed as the wounded skin can be （ ③ ） when a clot of blood is formed.

(a) 英文に最も合う見出しを次の1から4より選び、その番号を解答欄に記入しなさい。

1. Delivery of a Healing Agent to the Damaged Area

2. Engineers Inspired by the Human Blood Clotting System

3. Development of Self-healing Plastic

4. Development of a Polymer with Microscopic Capsules

(b) 下線部①に最も近い意味の文を次の1から4より選び、その番号を解答欄に記入しなさい。

1. 2014年に、技術者は人間の血液凝固因子の発見により、さらに広い穴をプラスチックで自動的に埋めることにしました。

2. 2014年に、人間の血液凝固系に発想を得た技術者は、さらに広い穴を自動的に埋めることのできるプラスチックを作り出しました

3. 2014年に、技術者は人間の血液凝固系を使い、さらに広い穴を自動的に埋めることのできるプラスチックを作り出しました。

4. 2014年に、血液凝固系により触発された技術者は、さらに広い穴が自動的に固まるプラスチックを作り出しました。

(c) 下線部②に最も近い意味を次の 1 から 4 より選び、その番号を解答欄に記入しなさい。

1. similar to
2. relative
3. relating to
4. seeming

(d) （　③　）に入る最適な語を次の 1 から 4 より選び、その番号を解答欄に記入しなさい。

1. healed
2. revealed
3. damaged
4. filled

Ⅶ　次の (a) から (f) について、各和文の意味を表すように 1 から 7 を並べかえて英文を作り、3 番目と 5 番目にくる語の番号を解答欄に記入しなさい。

(a) サーバが落ちたとき、データが失われたかもしれないと考え、皆慌てふためいた。

When the server went down, (1. because　2. panicked　3. have 4. disappeared　5. could　6. everyone　7. all the data).

(b) この論文は、強い風のもとで複数の球体が集合的にどのような動きをするかを的確に説明している。

This paper aptly (1. a　2. of　3. behaves　4. illustrates　5. spheres 6. group　7. how) collectively under strong wind.

(c) 科学者は、これらの遺伝子が、若年性の心臓病に関わる可能性の
あることを発見した。

Scientists discovered that (1. causing　2. genes　3. in　4. these
5. involved　6. may　7. be) early heart disease.

(d) その会社は、新規顧客のニーズを満たすために製品を変更するこ
とにした。

The company decided to modify their products (1. of　2. in　3. to
4. the　5. satisfy　6. order　7. needs) new customers.

(e) 今後50年間でロボットや機械が多くの人間の作業者に取って代わ
るだろう。

Over the next fifty years, (1. workers　2. by　3. will　4. many
5. replaced　6. be　7. human) robots and machines.

(f) 将来、地球のすべての化石燃料が使い果たされるとどうなるだろ
うか。

What will happen when (1. fuels　2. exhausted　3. all　4. fossil
5. earth's　6. the　7. are) in the future?

第 125 回 (2021. 1)

I　次の (a) から (j) の各英語について、最適な日本語を選び、その番号を解答欄に記入しなさい。

(a)　organ
　　　1.　器官
　　　2.　胞子
　　　3.　細菌

(b)　contradiction
　　　1.　変換
　　　2.　制限
　　　3.　矛盾

(c)　high-performance
　　　1.　高品質
　　　2.　高次元
　　　3.　高性能

(d)　distortion
　　　1.　変調
　　　2.　ひずみ
　　　3.　剛性

(e)　restructure
　　　1.　抑制する
　　　2.　再構築する
　　　3.　精製する

(f)　cavity
　　　1.　容器
　　　2.　空洞
　　　3.　真空

(g)　eventually
1. 辛うじて
2. 均一に
3. 結局は

(h)　insulation
1. 絶縁
2. 伝搬
3. 共振

(i)　solid line
1. 太線
2. 基線
3. 実線

(j)　moisture-proof
1. 耐熱の
2. 防寒の
3. 防湿の

Ⅱ　次の (a) から (j) の各日本語について、最適な英語を選び、その番号を解答欄に記入しなさい。

(a)　分散
1. proposition
2. hyperbola
3. dispersion

(b)　経度
1. latitude
2. equator
3. longitude

(c)　摩耗試験
1. acceptance test
2. preliminary test
3. wear test

(d) ヨウ素
$\left\{\begin{array}{l}\text{1. chlorine}\\\text{2. silicon}\\\text{3. iodine}\end{array}\right.$

(e) 妥当性
$\left\{\begin{array}{l}\text{1. rigidity}\\\text{2. validity}\\\text{3. integrity}\end{array}\right.$

(f) 対角線
$\left\{\begin{array}{l}\text{1. dashed line}\\\text{2. diagonal line}\\\text{3. base line}\end{array}\right.$

(g) 復元力
$\left\{\begin{array}{l}\text{1. encryption}\\\text{2. privilege}\\\text{3. resilience}\end{array}\right.$

(h) 周辺の
$\left\{\begin{array}{l}\text{1. rotary}\\\text{2. miscellaneous}\\\text{3. peripheral}\end{array}\right.$

(i) 取得する
$\left\{\begin{array}{l}\text{1. enclose}\\\text{2. acquire}\\\text{3. penetrate}\end{array}\right.$

(j) 余剰
$\left\{\begin{array}{l}\text{1. surplus}\\\text{2. ellipse}\\\text{3. intake}\end{array}\right.$

Ⅲ　次の (a) から (d) の英語の説明に対応する語を下の 1 から 10 より選び、その番号を解答欄に記入しなさい。なお、 1 から 10 は 1 回しか使えない。

(a) A rectangular array of numbers, algebraic symbols, or mathematical functions, especially when such arrays are added and multiplied according to certain rules

(b) The amount of a substance or object that is shown by the relation of its mass or weight to its volume

(c) A chemical used for killing animals or insects that damage plants or crops

(d) Any electronic device, such as a microphone, that changes one form of energy into another

1. regulator　　2. solvent　　3. matrix　　4. pesticide

5. thickness　　6. cube　　7. density　　8. transducer

9. volume　　10. sequence

Ⅳ　次の (a) から (d) の各組の英文が同じ意味になるよう、（　）に入れる
　　最適な語を下の 1 から 10 より選び、その番号を解答欄に記入しなさい。
　　なお、1 から 10 は 1 回しか使えない。文頭に来るべき語であっても先
　　頭は小文字になっている。

(a)　As another option, you can click the question mark icon to
　　　access the Help window.

　　　(　　　　), you can click the question mark icon to access
　　　the Help window.

(b)　The temperature in the room is too high because the air does
　　　not circulate properly.

　　　The temperature in the room is too high because of
　　　improper (　　　　).

(c)　The scientist discovered that the ground contains a lot of gold.

　　　The scientist discovered that the ground is (　　　　) in gold.

(d)　Methanol changes into a gas at a lower temperature than water.

　　　Methanol (　　　　) at a lower temperature than water.

1.　migration　　2.　evaporates　　3.　feasibility　　4.　rusty

5.　ventilation　　6.　abundant　　7.　separately　　8.　negative

9.　alternatively　　10. removes

V　次の (a) から (h) の英文を完成させる語として、最適なものをそれぞ
れの 1 から 4 より選び、その番号を解答欄に記入しなさい。

(a)　We have to lease several machines (1. because　2. however
　　 3. without　4. although) the ones we bought will not arrive until
　　 next month.

(b)　The company, (1. each　2. despite　3. until　4. whose) new
　　 product lines are very popular, has become a major player in the
　　 industry.

(c)　Proteins are organic (1. molecules　2. compounds　3. atoms
　　 4. matters) that consist of amino acids joined by peptide bonds.

(d)　The (1. amplitude　2. speed　3. direction　4. frequency) of a
　　 sound wave is the number of vibration cycles within a set period
　　 of time.

(e)　This book explains how these birds (1. adapt　2. adopt　3. addict
　　 4. conflict) themselves to new environment.

(f)　The doctor recommended that my son be (1. injected　2. donated
　　 3. consumed　4. solved) with the flu vaccine as soon as possible.

(g)　Electrical outlets have been placed (1. many　2. some　3. by
　　 4. every) two meters along the corridor of each floor of the
　　 building.

(h)　In the periodic table, elements are (1. arranged　2. arranging
　　 3. extracted　4. extracting) in periods and groups.

Ⅵ　次の英文を読んで、各設問に答えなさい。

Many inventors have modeled machines after animals throughout the centuries. Copying from nature has (　①　) advantages. Most living creatures now on the earth are the product of two billion years of evolution, and the construction of machines to work in an environment resembling that of living creatures can profit from ② this enormous experience. ③ Although the easiest way may be thought to be direct imitation of nature, this is often difficult if not impossible, among other reasons because of the difference in scale. Bionics researchers have found that it is more advantageous to understand the principles of why things work in nature than to copy its details.

(a) 英文に最も合う見出しを、次の 1 から 4 より選び、その番号を解答欄に記入しなさい。

1.　How to Recreate Animals and Nature Mechanically

2.　How Animals Evolved on the Earth

3.　The Ethics of Bionics Researchers

4.　Humans' Approach to Mimicking Nature

(b) (　①　) に入る最も適切な語を次の 1 から 4 より選び、その番号を解答欄に記入しなさい。

1.　huge

2.　total

3.　lots

4.　attached

(c) 下線部③に最も近い意味の文を次の 1 から 4 より選び、その番号を解答欄に記入しなさい。

1. 最も簡単な方法は自然をそのまま取り入れることだが、時にはそのスケールの大きさから取り入れることは不可能ではないにしろ難しいこともある。

2. 最も簡単な方法は自然をそのまま製品に取り入れることだが、製品と自然界のスケールが合うことがほとんどなく、実現は不可能である。

3. 最も簡単な方法は自然界をそのまま真似すればよいと思われがちだが、スケールが合わない場合は難しく、あった場合でも不可能なことが多い。

4. 最も簡単な方法は自然界をそのまま真似すればよいと思われがちだが、スケールが違うなどといった理由で非常に難しいか不可能に近いこともある。

(d) 下線部②の this enormous experience が文中で何を意味しているのかを次の 1 から 4 より選び、その番号を解答欄に記入しなさい。

1. 生体工学者たちのこれまでの経験や知識
2. 自然界を真似ようとして試行錯誤してきた経験と知識
3. 生物界の 20 億年に及ぶ進化
4. 生物界の特徴を分析してきたこと

Ⅶ　次の (a) から (f) について、各和文の意味を表すように 1 から 7 を並べかえて英文を作り、3 番目と 5 番目にくる語の番号を解答欄に記入しなさい。

(a) あらゆる科学現象を物理学のみで説明するのは非常に難しい。

It is very difficult (1. explain　2. scientific　3. to　4. through 5. every　6. phenomenon　7. solely) physics.

(b) 新たに開発された制御システムにより消費電力を約 30％削減することができる。

The newly (1. can　2. developed　3. energy　4. by　5. reduce 6. control system　7. use) about 30%.

(c) 高速列車の中には、最高速度が時速 300km を超えるものがある。

Some high-speed trains (1. than　2. of　3. have　4. speed　5. a 6. more　7. maximum) 300 km per hour.

(d) 古代には火星が深さ 137m の水で覆われていたという強力な証拠がある。

There (1. evidence　2. strong　3. was　4. that　5. is　6. covered 7. Mars) with water 137 meters deep in ancient times.

(e) サイトが暗号化されているかどうか判断するには、URL の始めの 「https」を探します。

Look for "https" at the beginning of a URL (1. the　2. determine 3. is　4. whether　5. to　6. encrypted　7. website).

(f) 球体は常にどこから見ても正確な円形の輪郭を持っているように見える。

A sphere always appears to have a completely round (1. look 2. wherever　3. from　4. it　5. you　6. outline　7. at).

第 124 回（2020. 11）

I　次の (a) から (j) の各英語について、最適な日本語を選び、その番号
を解答欄に記入しなさい。

(a)　infinite
1. 不燃性の
2. 無限の
3. 無視できる

(b)　brass
1. 真鍮
2. 石灰
3. 水銀

(c)　fragmentation
1. 平均化
2. 断片化
3. 多重化

(d)　variable
1. 変数
2. 変調
3. 特質

(e)　supplement
1. 吸い込む
2. 貫通する
3. 補足する

(f)　fuel gauge
1. 液体燃料
2. 発熱量
3. 燃料計

(g) arrowhead
- 1. 許可
- 2. 矢じり
- 3. 射程

(h) general-purpose
- 1. 汎用性
- 2. 専門性
- 3. 実用性

(i) vicinity
- 1. 上側
- 2. 場所
- 3. 付近

(j) significance
- 1. 安定性
- 2. 互換性
- 3. 重要性

Ⅱ 次の (a) から (j) の各日本語について、最適な英語を選び、その番号を解答欄に記入しなさい。

(a) 媒介物
- 1. intermedium
- 2. fluid
- 3. impurity

(b) 組織
- 1. asset
- 2. tissue
- 3. dew

(c) 変更
- 1. compensation
- 2. modification
- 3. substitution

(d)　保持する
- 1. invent
- 2. form
- 3. retain

(e)　粘度
- 1. viscosity
- 2. friction
- 3. purification

(f)　省略
- 1. extraction
- 2. omission
- 3. rejection

(g)　一時的に
- 1. thoroughly
- 2. temporarily
- 3. instantly

(h)　二次方程式
- 1. quadratic equation
- 2. linear equation
- 3. square root

(i)　強度
- 1. reciprocal
- 2. yield
- 3. intensity

(j)　定格の
- 1. appropriate
- 2. focal
- 3. rated

Ⅲ　次の (a) から (d) の英語の説明に対応する語を下の 1 から 10 より選び、その番号を解答欄に記入しなさい。なお、1 から 10 は 1 回しか使えない。

(a) An instruction written by a physician that authorizes a patient to be issued with a medicine

(b) A material or substance that is used to prevent heat, electricity, or sound from going into or out of something

(c) A graphic symbol on a computer display screen that represents an application, an object, or a function

(d) An infective agent that typically consists of a nucleic acid molecule in a protein coat and is able to multiply only within the living cells of a host

1. enzyme　　　　2. dial　　　3. icon　　　　4. insulation

5. perception　　6. filler　　7. subscription　8. prescription

9. semiconductor　10. virus

Ⅳ 次の (a) から (d) の各組の英文が同じ意味になるよう、( ) に入れる
　 最適な語を下の 1 から 10 より選び、その番号を解答欄に記入しなさい。
　 なお、1 から 10 は 1 回しか使えない。

(a) 　Aluminum can be combined with additive elements to form
　　 several different kinds of alloys.

　　 Aluminum can be combined with additive elements to
　　 form (　　　) alloys.

(b) 　The cables designed for this product cannot be substituted with
　　 other similar cables.

　　 The cables designed for this product are not (　　　) with
　　 other similar cables.

(c) 　The object does not move because the forces acting on it are
　　 balanced.

　　 The object is in a state of (　　　).

(d) 　The researchers estimate that the island's mammoths became
　　 extinct roughly 5,000 years ago.

　　 The researchers estimate that the island's mammoths (　　　)
　　 roughly 5,000 years ago.

1.　specific　　　2.　equilibrium　　3.　disappeared　4.　volatility

5.　summarized　　6.　incompatible　7.　numerical　　8.　various

9.　interchangeable 10. revealed

V 次の (a) から (h) の英文を完成させる語として、最適なものをそれぞれの 1 から 4 より選び、その番号を解答欄に記入しなさい。

(a) The company is developing unmanned aircraft, but is currently facing several (1. unexpected　2. uncourageous　3. unleash　4. unveil) technical problems.

(b) The budget for this project is very (1. irritated　2. sorrow　3. borrow　4. limited), so it might not be successful.

(c) Good conductors, which have very low resistance, (1. give　2. provide　3. allow　4. make) large currents to flow through them.

(d) Two hydrogen atoms and one oxygen atom are bonded to (1. call　2. form　3. move　4. activate) a water molecule.

(e) It is said that many forms of cancers can be cured if they are (1. linked　2. knotted　3. detected　4. disclosed) early.

(f) The internal (1. structure　2. planet　3. frame　4. partition) of Mars has been investigated by scientists.

(g) Some fungi look like plants but they cannot create energy from sunlight (1. as　2. because　3.so　4. that) plants do.

(h) The car accident occurred (1. rarely　2. just　3. especially　4. reluctantly) as the driver was distracted by his smartphone while driving.

Ⅵ　次の英文を読んで、各設問に答えなさい。

① Hydrogen fuel cell vehicles (FCVs) are similar to electric vehicles (EVs) in that they use an electric motor instead of an internal combustion engine to power the wheels. However, while EVs run on batteries that must be plugged in to recharge, FCVs generate their electricity ② onboard. In a fuel cell, hydrogen (H_2) gas from the vehicle fuel tank combines with oxygen (O_2) from the air to generate electricity (③) only water and heat as byproducts of the process.

(a) 英文に最も合う見出しを、次の 1 から 4 より選び、その番号を解答欄に記入しなさい。

1.　How Hydrogen Fuel Cell Vehicles Generate Electricity
2.　How to Differentiate Hydrogen Fuel Cell Vehicles from Electric Vehicles
3.　Environmentally-friendly Hydrogen Fuel Cell Vehicle
4.　How to Recharge Fuel Cell Vehicles

(b) 下線部①に最も近い意味の文を次の 1 から 4 より選び、その番号を解答欄に記入しなさい。

1.　水素燃料自動車は電気自動車と同様に、電気モータを利用して内燃エンジンのように車輪を動かす。

2.　水素燃料自動車は電気自動車と同様に、電気モータが内燃エンジンのように車輪を動かす。

3.　水素燃料自動車が電気自動車と同様に、内燃エンジンではなく電気モータを用いて車輪を動かす。

4.　内燃エンジン自動車は電気モータを使わないが、水素燃料自動車や電気自動車と同じように車輪を動かすのは同じである。

(c) 下線部②の語を言い換えるのに最適な語を次の 1 から 4 より選び、その番号を解答欄に記入しなさい。

1. while running
2. during operation
3. on circuit boards
4. in the vehicles

(d) （　③　）に入る最適な語を次の 1 から 4 より選び、その番号を解答欄に記入しなさい。

1. with
2. which
3. so
4. after

Ⅶ　次の (a) から (f) について、各和文の意味を表すように 1 から 7 を並べかえて英文を作り、3 番目と 5 番目にくる語の番号を解答欄に記入しなさい。

(a) 朝食を抜かすのは健康によくなく、体重増加につながると言われている。

It is said (1. is　2. can　3. skipping　4. unhealthy　5. breakfast　6. and　7. that) cause weight gain.

(b) この新型航空機は非常に軽量で、燃費も良いため、長距離路線に使われることになるだろう。

The new aircraft is (1. that　2. light　3. and　4. fuel-efficient　5. will　6. it　7. so) be used in long-haul routes.

(c) 心臓移植は最も難しい手術の一つと言われており、細心の注意の
もとに行われる。

A heart transplant is considered as one of the (1. and　2. difficult
3. under　4. performed　5. surgeries　6. most　7. is) extreme
caution.

(d) 顕微鏡の総合倍率は、その個別のレンズの倍率の積である。

The total magnification of a microscope (1. a product　2. is　3. of
4. the　5. its　6. magnification of　7. individual) lenses.

(e) 開発途上国の主な課題の一つは、人々に安全な飲料水を供給する
ことである。

A major problem (1. to　2. is　3. in　4. with　5. the developing countries
6. people　7. provide) safe drinking water.

(f) 平均値とは、数値の和をその個数で割ったものである。

The (1. the　2. the numerical values　3. mean　4. sum　5. divided
6. of　7. is) by the number of the values.

第 122 回（2020.1）

I　次の (a) から (j) の各英語について、最適な日本語を選び、その番号を解答欄に記入しなさい。

(a) modulation
1. 伝搬
2. 増幅
3. 変調

(b) spillway
1. 放水路
2. 進路
3. 伝送路

(c) turbulence
1. 発光性
2. 推進力
3. 乱流

(d) torsional strength
1. せん断強さ
2. 引っ張り強さ
3. ねじり強さ

(e) presence
1. 存在
2. 提案
3. 準備

(f) slightly
1. ほとんど
2. わずかに
3. 適当に

(g) oblique line
- 1. 切断線
- 2. 破線
- 3. 斜線

(h) epidemic
- 1. 抗生物質
- 2. 免疫
- 3. 流行病

(i) perpetual motion
- 1. 往復運動
- 2. 物体運動
- 3. 永久運動

(j) astronaut
- 1. 宇宙研究者
- 2. 宇宙飛行士
- 3. 宇宙学者

Ⅱ　次の (a) から (j) の各日本語について、最適な英語を選び、その番号を解答欄に記入しなさい。

(a) 天頂角
- 1. zenith angle
- 2. elevation angle
- 3. altitude angle

(b) 利得
- 1. grain
- 2. grid
- 3. gain

(c) 加入する
- 1. mount
- 2. subscribe
- 3. bundle

(d) 融点

- 1. boiling point
- 2. freezing point
- 3. melting point

(e) 振動

- 1. revolution
- 2. vibration
- 3. insulation

(f) 多様な

- 1. scanty
- 2. mature
- 3. diverse

(g) 不確実性

- 1. deficiency
- 2. uncertainty
- 3. nonequivalence

(h) 人工知能

- 1. advanced intelligence
- 2. arithmetical intelligence
- 3. artificial intelligence

(i) 監督する

- 1. supervise
- 2. approve
- 3. perceive

(j) X 軸

- 1. X-column
- 2. X-axis
- 3. X-index

Ⅲ　次の (a) から (d) の英語の説明に対応する語を下の 1 から 10 より選び、その番号を解答欄に記入しなさい。なお、 1 から 10 は 1 回しか使えない。

(a) A very violent tropical storm found in the West Pacific Ocean

(b) A series of steps, especially in a computer program, which will give you the answer to a specific question

(c) A chemical reaction that uses oxygen to produce light and heat

(d) An optical instrument used for magnifying minute objects

1.　formula　　　2.　combustion　3.　tornado　　　4.　diffusion

5.　loop　　　　6.　telescope　　7.　typhoon　　　8.　stabilizer

9.　algorithm　　10. microscope

Ⅳ　次の (a) から (d) の各組の英文が同じ意味になるよう、(　) に入れる
　最適な語を下の 1 から 10 より選び、その番号を解答欄に記入しなさい。
　なお、1 から 10 は 1 回しか使えない。

(a) 　The risk of human errors including a typing error should be
　　　reduced to the lowest possible level.

　　　The risk of human errors including a typing error should
　　　be (　　　　).

(b) 　Water in the air can be taken in by cactuses in desert environments.

　　　Cactuses can (　　　　) water in the air in desert environments.

(c) 　Due to proper maintenance, this machine works very well and
　　　rarely breaks down.

　　　Due to proper maintenance, this machine is (　　　　).

(d) 　The International Space Station utilizes the energy of the sun
　　　to supply power.

　　　The International Space Station utilizes (　　　　) energy to
　　　supply power.

1. sunny 　　2. discharge 　　3. minimized 　4. solar

5. compatible 6. manipulated 　7. lunar 　　　8. reliable

9. migrated 　10. absorb

V 次の (a) から (h) の英文を完成させる語として、最適なものをそれぞれの 1 から 4 より選び、その番号を解答欄に記入しなさい。

(a) I have not yet written the report, nor (1. will　2. when　3. are　4. which) I until I finish the final experiment.

(b) The sea in this area occasionally freezes (1. at　2. on　3. in　4. when) February, and some sea ice remains all year.

(c) (1. Each　2. Every　3. Another　4. All) servers have to be installed in an air-conditioned computer room because they consume large power and generate a lot of heat.

(d) You can find the area of a rectangle by (1. making　2. specifying　3. multiplying　4. dividing) the length by the width.

(e) Lines of (1. latitude　2. longitude　3. meridian　4. horizon) run around the earth horizontally and parallel to the equator.

(f) People with spinal cord injuries have trouble (1. maintaining　2. changing　3. tripping　4. creating) balance when they are not using the harness.

(g) DNA is the molecule that holds (1. fossil　2. organic　3. vertical　4. genetic) information passed on from one generation to the next.

(h) If you use a password easy to guess, an attacker will easily crack it using an (1. automatic　2. inaccessible 3. incompatible　4. inconsistent) procedure.

Ⅵ　次の英文を読んで、各設問に答えなさい。

Both people and animals sense the world around them in various ways. They can see, hear, feel, smell, or taste. However, what about plants? They do not have eyes, ears, skin, a nose or a mouth like us, but they may have their own (　①　). For example, the sunflower senses light so that it can turn toward the sun. Furthermore, perhaps surprisingly, scientists think that a plant called dodder has a sense of smell. The dodder does not grow roots and cannot even create energy for itself. Instead,　② it attaches itself to a tomato plant and takes nutrients from the plant.　③ Dodder plants sense chemicals in the air that other plants release, and smell the tomato as their prey.

(a) 英文に最も合う見出しを次の1から4より選び、その番号を解答欄に記入しなさい。

1.　Can a Plant Smell?
2.　Using All Five Senses
3.　How to Grow Dodders
4.　Tomatoes Smell Their Prey

(b) (　①　) に入る最適な語を次の1から4より選び、その番号を解答欄に記入しなさい。

1.　possessions
2.　equivalents
3.　portions
4.　territories

(c) 下線部②は文中の何をさしているか、最適な語を次の 1 から 4 より選び、その番号を解答欄に記入しなさい。

1.　energy

2.　a sense of smell

3.　the dodder

4.　a root

(d) 下線部③に最も近い意味の文を次の 1 から 4 より選び、その番号を解答欄に記入しなさい。

1.　ネナシカズラは、獲物のトマトの臭いを察知するために、他の植物が空気中に放出した化学物質を吸収する。

2.　ネナシカズラは、他の植物に向けて空気中に化学物質を放出し、獲物のトマトをおびきよせる。

3.　ネナシカズラは、他の植物が空気中に放った化学物質を吸収し、獲物のトマトと同じ臭いを出す。

4.　ネナシカズラは、他の植物が放出した空気中の化学物質を察知し、獲物のトマトの臭いもかぎつける。

Ⅶ　次の (a) から (f) について、各和文の意味を表すように 1 から 7 を並べかえて英文を作り、3 番目と 5 番目にくる語の番号を解答欄に記入しなさい。

(a) バルブで流量を調整することで、エアシリンダーの速度を制御することができる。

You can control (1. with　2. the flow rate　3. a valve 4. the pneumatic cylinder　5. by　6. the speed of　7. adjusting).

(b) この新開発のスキャナーは以前のモデルよりもずっと使いやすい。

This newly developed (1. is　2. user-friendly　3. much　4. than 5. the previous　6. scanner　7. more) model.

(c) この研究は、脂肪の多い食事と心臓病の高い発症率が関係していることを示している。

This study shows that (1. high　2. associated　3. a　4. are　5. fatty 6. with　7. diets) rate of heart disease.

(d) 物質の密度は、単位体積当たりの質量と定義される。

The density of a material (1. its　2. per　3. as　4. is　5. mass 6. unit volume　7. defined).

(e) スーパーコンピュータの資金調達は、コンピュータ科学の他の分野に遅れをとった。

The (1. other　2. fell　3. for　4. funding　5. supercomputers 6. areas　7. behind) of computer science.

(f) あなたが先週始めた実験の進捗状況を逐次報告してください。

Please keep (1. the status of　2. started　3. me　4. you 5. the experiment　6. informed　7. of) last week.

I　次の (a) から (j) の各英語について、最適な日本語を選び、その番号
　　を解答欄に記入しなさい。

(a)　precision
- 1. 明瞭さ
- 2. 精密さ
- 3. 便利さ

(b)　fluorescent paint
- 1. 蛍光塗料
- 2. 錆止め塗料
- 3. 抗菌性塗料

(c)　universal joint
- 1. 標準継ぎ手
- 2. 耐熱継ぎ手
- 3. 自在継ぎ手

(d)　wind
- 1. 回収する
- 2. 閉じる
- 3. 巻く

(e)　assumption
- 1. 達成
- 2. 仮定
- 3. 同化

(f)　tilt
- 1. 曲げ
- 2. 旋回
- 3. 傾き

(g) lightproof
  1. 透光性の
  2. 偏光性の
  3. 遮光性の

(h) production process
  1. 検査工程
  2. 製造工程
  3. 開発工程

(i) threshold
  1. 実効値
  2. 近似値
  3. 閾値

(j) detached
  1. 分離した
  2. 直立した
  3. 安定した

Ⅱ　次の (a) から (j) の各日本語について、最適な英語を選び、その番号を解答欄に記入しなさい。

(a) 変数
  1. variable
  2. coefficient
  3. fraction

(b) 外乱
  1. fission
  2. reflection
  3. disturbance

(c) 均一に
  1. firmly
  2. briefly
  3. evenly

(d)　3 分の 2
  1. three two
  2. two-three
  3. two-thirds

(e)　区別
  1. distillation
  2. distinction
  3. deviation

(f)　染色体
  1. gene
  2. organ
  3. chromosome

(g)　安全規格
  1. safety means
  2. safety manual
  3. safety standards

(h)　降ろす
  1. alter
  2. fall
  3. lower

(i)　糸
  1. thread
  2. kiln
  3. vinyl

(j)　直流
  1. direct ampere
  2. direct current
  3. direct circuit

Ⅲ 次の (a) から (d) の英語の説明に対応する語を下の 1 から 10 より選び、その番号を解答欄に記入しなさい。なお、1 から 10 は 1 回しか使えない。

(a) A natural number greater than 1 that cannot be formed by multiplying two smaller natural numbers

(b) A document or computer program that calculates numbers in columns and rows

(c) The act of injecting an antigen to prevent diseases

(d) The force that makes it difficult for one object to slide on the surface of another object

1. vaccination　　2. cell　　　　3. friction　　4. ventilation

5. real number　　6. convection　7. inertia　　8. irrigation

9. prime number　10. spreadsheet

Ⅳ　次の (a) から (d) の各組の英文が同じ意味になるよう、( ) に入れる
最適な語を下の 1 から 10 より選び、その番号を解答欄に記入しなさい。
なお、1 から 10 は 1 回しか使えない。文頭に来るべき語であっても先
頭は小文字になっている。

(a) 　In a mixed-model assembly line, many models are produced at
the same time.

In a mixed-model assembly line, many models are produced
(　　　).

(b) 　Serious harm may be caused by unwanted objects coming from
outside.

(　　　) objects may cause serious harm.

(c) 　The solubility of an alcohol in water changes with its
molecular weight.

The molecular weight of an alcohol (　　　) its solubility in
water.

(d) 　The doctor studies medicines that kill bacteria and cure infections.

The doctor studies (　　　).

1. dissolves　2. protruding　3. affects　4. concurrently

5. foreign　6. antibiotics　7. statistically　8. inherent

9. germs　10. consequently

V　次の (a) から (h) の英文を完成させる語として、最適なものをそれぞれの 1 から 4 より選び、その番号を解答欄に記入しなさい。

(a)　Many scientists say that although the movie is entertaining, it (1. concludes　2. agrees　3. consists　4. contains) a major mistake from a scientific point of view.

(b)　Our oil sources may be exhausted in the future, so (1. exchangeable 2. replaceable　3. alternative　4. continuous) energy sources need to be developed.

(c)　We could see the microbes magnified 6000 times under the (1. modulator　2. telescope　3. microscope　4. microammeter).

(d)　Use electrical shocks to (1. interrupt　2. secrete　3. intercept 4. activate) the nerve cells of paralyzed rats and to cure them.

(e)　This mobile battery (1. holds　2. runs　3. turns　4. leaves) enough power to charge my smartphone more than three times.

(f)　A tightened guitar string produces a higher note because its natural (1. density　2. length　3. frequency　4. pressure) becomes higher.

(g)　Air bags (1. inflate　2. relieve　3. shrink　4. widen) in a crash to prevent the passengers from hitting the steering wheel and windshield.

(h)　The optical fibers used for high-speed data transfer rely on the properties of light and its reflection at a (1. boundary 2. deviation　3. friction　4. parabola) between two types of matter.

VI　次の英文を読んで、各設問に答えなさい。

Researchers developed a treated cotton for use in a self-cleaning cloth. The handy fabric gets its self-cleaning abilities from a chemical mixture that coats the cotton threads. The coating includes two substances known as photocatalysts, which (①) chemical reactions in sunlight. One is called titanium dioxide*, which is generally used to help sunscreen protect your skin. The other, called silver iodide**, is often used for developing photographs.

Researchers have previously shown that ② titanium dioxide mixtures can remove stains in clothes—but with exposure to ultraviolet, not visible, light. The waves of ultraviolet light have more energy than visible light, and their wavelengths are (③). Other studies have demonstrated that silver iodide can speed up chemical reactions in sunlight. So the researchers combined the two photocatalysts to exploit their properties.

［注］titanium dioxide*: 二酸化チタン　　iodide**: ヨウ化物

(a) 英文に最も合う見出しを、次の 1 から 4 より選び、その番号を解答欄に記入しなさい。

1.　Light Starts the Chemical Reaction

2.　Handy Photocatalyst Used for Fabric

3.　Silver Iodide Speeds up Reactions in Sunlight

4.　A New Self-Cleaning Cloth

(b) (①) に入る最も適切な語を次の 1 から 4 より選び、その番号を解答欄に記入しなさい。

1.　inhibit

2.　slow

3.　make

4.　promote

(c) 下線部②に最も近い意味の文を次の 1 から 4 より選び、その番号を解答欄に記入しなさい。

1. 二酸化チタン混合物は、紫外線ではなく可視光線にさらすと、衣類の汚れがとれる。

2. 二酸化チタン混合物で衣類の汚れをとるが、紫外線にさらした場合、可視光線にはさらさない。

3. 二酸化チタン化合物は、紫外線にさらした状態で衣類の汚れをとるので、可視光線はいらない。

4. 二酸化チタン混合物は、可視光線ではなく紫外線にさらすと、衣類の汚れがとれる。

(d) （　③　）に入る最適な語を次の 1 から 4 より選び、その番号を解答欄に記入しなさい。

1. higher
2. lighter
3. shorter
4. brighter

Ⅶ　次の (a) から (f) について、各和文の意味を表すように 1 から 7 を並べかえて英文を作り、3 番目と 5 番目にくる語の番号を解答欄に記入しなさい。

(a) パーツが適合しないと分かったら、どなたと連絡を取ればいいでしょうか。

Could (1. who　2. contact　3. should　4. me　5. I　6. tell　7. you) if I find out that the parts do not fit?

(b) このシステムでは、検査データは 15 分ごとにクラウドに自動保存
される。

The system automatically (1. to　2. 15-minute　3. at　4. saves
5. inspection　6. cloud storage　7. data) intervals.

(c) その気象衛星は、時速 1600 キロで地球を周回している。

The weather satellite (1. earth　2. at　3. the　4. orbits　5. speed
6. a　7. of) 1600 kilometers an hour.

(d) 鉛蓄電池は、電気自動車に使うには重すぎる。

Lead-acid batteries (1. too　2. in　3. be　4. used　5. to　6. are
7. heavy) electric vehicles.

(e) これらのカプセルの直径は、50 〜 100 ミクロンの範囲でばらつき
がある。

The (1. these capsules　2. in　3. 50 to 100　4. of　5. diameters
6. vary　7. the range of) microns.

(f) 水蒸気が開口部から出てくるように、フラスコを加熱してください。

Heat (1. come　2. the flask　3. water vapor　4. so　5. will　6. out
7. that) of the opening.

第120回（2019.7）

Ⅰ 次の (a) から (j) の各英語について、最適な日本語を選び、その番号を解答欄に記入しなさい。

(a) contraction
- 1. 飽和
- 2. 過熱
- 3. 収縮

(b) fiber
- 1. 触媒
- 2. 脂肪
- 3. 繊維

(c) crude oil
- 1. 潤滑油
- 2. 原油
- 3. 石油

(d) alternative
- 1. 実質の
- 2. 代替の
- 3. 例年の

(e) lava
- 1. 溶岩
- 2. 水晶
- 3. 胞子

(f) equation
- 1. 平等
- 2. 等式
- 3. 等号

(g) cross section
- 1. 境界面
- 2. 斜面
- 3. 断面

(h) sustain
- 1. 持続させる
- 2. かき混ぜる
- 3. ひっくり返す

(i) unglazed
- 1. 無効の
- 2. 地熱の
- 3. 素焼きの

(j) perpetual motion
- 1. 往復運動
- 2. 永久運動
- 3. 物体運動

Ⅱ　次の (a) から (j) の各日本語について、最適な英語を選び、その番号を解答欄に記入しなさい。

(a) 復号器
- 1. coder
- 2. repeater
- 3. decoder

(b) 療法
- 1. fatigue
- 2. therapy
- 3. infection

(c) 利用
- 1. inauguration
- 2. activation
- 3. utilization

(d) 潜在的な
- 1. periodical
- 2. potential
- 3. proportional

(e) 欠陥
- 1. objective
- 2. defective
- 3. suspect

(f) 視点
- 1. proposition
- 2. viewpoint
- 3. dialog

(g) 界面
- 1. interface
- 2. obstacle
- 3. tolerance

(h) 保有する
- 1. possess
- 2. facilitate
- 3. manipulate

(i) 構成要素
- 1. manuscript
- 2. equilibrium
- 3. constituent

(j) ナトリウム
- 1. iodine
- 2. nitrogen
- 3. sodium

Ⅲ　次の (a) から (d) の英語の説明に対応する語を下の 1 から 10 より選び、その番号を解答欄に記入しなさい。なお、1 から 10 は 1 回しか使えない。

(a) A two-terminal electronic component that conducts current primarily in one direction

(b) An abnormal growth of cells which tend to proliferate in an uncontrolled way

(c) Mathematical symbols that tell you to do addition or subtraction inside them first

(d) The gradual destruction and removal of rock or soil by natural forces such as water, wind, or ice

1. erosion　　　2. flood　　　3. calculators　　4. deposition

5. swelling　　 6. brackets　　7. diode　　　　8. statistics

9. cancer　　　10. triode

Ⅳ　次の (a) から (d) の各組の英文が同じ意味になるよう、（　）に入れる
最適な語を下の 1 から 10 より選び、その番号を解答欄に記入しなさい。
なお、1 から 10 は 1 回しか使えない。

(a)　You need to exercise extreme caution when storing or handling
hazardous materials and liquids that catch fire easily.

You need to exercise extreme caution when storing or handling
hazardous materials and (　　　　) liquids.

(b)　The previous record, set in 1990, was broken by the 574 km/h
record.

The 574 km/h record (　　　　) the earlier record set in 1990.

(c)　Almost no visible signs of volcanic activity were observed a
year ago.

There were (　　　　) visible signs of volcanic activity a year
ago.

(d)　Copper is a ductile metal and often used to manufacture thin
wires.

Copper, (　　　　) is a ductile metal, is often used to manufacture
thin wires.

1. over　　　2. accessible　　　3. won　　　4. degradable

5. few　　　6. flammable　　　7. which　　　8. many

9. what　　　10. broke

V　次の (a) から (h) の英文を完成させる語として、最適なものをそれぞ
れの 1 から 4 より選び、その番号を解答欄に記入しなさい。

(a)　The temperature became lower (1. as　2. with　3. which
4. during) we approached the top of the mountain.

(b)　Even a sophisticated computer (1. had better　2. be　3. can　4. is)
malfunction, so we have to prepare a contingency plan.

(c)　At a glance, the results of the two experiments seemed (1. difference
2. identical　3. different　4. identity), but we found them to be
the same after detailed examinations.

(d)　In this country, the birthrate is rapidly (1. declining　2. turning
3. depending　4. sharing) while the population of elderly people
is growing.

(e)　The crust of the earth is about ten kilometers (1. long　2. flat
3. wide　4. thick) under the ocean.

(f)　A stroke is a sudden blockage or breaking of a blood vessel
(1. resulting from　2. due to　3. resulting in　4. because of) loss
of consciousness or speech.

(g)　Distilled water is made by heating water until it becomes (1. vapor
2. ice　3. solid　4. gel) and then cooling it down.

(h)　In physics, all materials consist of tiny, moving (1. muscles
2. crystals　3. particles　4. chemicals) called atoms, ions and
molecules.

VI　次の英文を読んで、各設問に答えなさい。

Deep learning is a form of machine learning done by a computer programmed to gain "(　①　)" from performing tasks. Through deep learning, a computer system processes a large amount of data, which it can then use to make decisions about other data. Basically, ② it allows computers to make decisions based on information they already have, much like the human mind does.
One of the main applications of machines that utilize deep learning is ③ data recognition. Such machines would help people in many situations: communicating using speech recognition, finding objects or people through image recognition, and identifying causes of diseases in patients.

(a) 英文に最も合う見出しを、次の1から4より選び、その番号を解答欄に記入しなさい。

1. Deep Learning May Overcome Human Mind

2. Based on Data Recognition

3. The Future of Deep Learning

4. Deep Learning for Decision-Making by Computers

(b) (　①　) に入る最も適切な語句を次の1から4より選び、その番号を解答欄に記入しなさい。

1. feelings

2. experience

3. perfection

4. fantasy

(c) 下線部②に最も近い意味を次の1から4より選び、その番号を解答欄に記入しなさい。

1. これでコンピュータは、人間の知性そっくりに、既に持っている情報に基づいて判断できるようになる。

2. コンピュータが既に有している情報に基づいて決断をくだせるのは、まるで人間の意志のようだ。

3. これでコンピュータは、人間の意のままに、既に持っている情報に基づいて判断できるようになる。

4. コンピュータが決断を下せるように、人間の知性にあるような既にそこにある情報をベースにする。

(d) 下線部③の例として本文に挙げられていないものを次の1から4より選び、その番号を解答欄に記入しなさい。

1. 人の顔を見分ける

2. 病気の原因を特定する

3. 臭いを嗅ぎ分ける

4. 話し言葉を聞き分ける

Ⅶ　次の (a) から (f) について、各和文の意味を表すように1から7を並べかえて英文を作り、3番目と5番目にくる語の番号を解答欄に記入しなさい。

(a) 全ての改修作業は、年内には終わっているはずだ。

All (1. by　2. been　3. the　4. have　5. completed　6. will　7. refurbishments) the end of the year.

(b) ガラスのリサイクル工程では、ガラスを色ごとに選別してから、洗浄して、不純物を取り除く。

In the glass recycling process, glass is sorted by (1. it　2. before 3. remove　4. to　5. washed　6. is　7. color) impurities.

(c) システムエラーのために、多くの人への支払いが予定通りにされなかった。

Many people (1. not　2. were　3. on　4. because　5. paid　6. of 7. time) the system error.

(d) このテープは、長期間日光にさらされると粘着力がなくなる。

This tape will (1. sunlight　2. exposed　3. adhesiveness　4. lose 5. its　6. if　7. to) for a long time.

(e) 半透明の素材は、ある程度の光を通過させる。

A translucent material (1. light　2. through　3. some　4. it　5. to 6. allows　7. pass).

(f) 先行技術調査は、特許申請をすべきか否かを判断するのに役立つ。

Prior-art search (1. apply　2. to　3. will　4. whether　5. decide 6. you　7. help) for a patent or not.

第 119 回（2019. 5）

I　次の (a) から (j) の各英語について、最適な日本語を選び、その番号を解答欄に記入しなさい。

(a)　induce
1. 連結する
2. 識別する
3. 誘発する

(b)　convex lens
1. 凹レンズ
2. 凸レンズ
3. 単眼レンズ

(c)　resources
1. 能力
2. 環境
3. 資源

(d)　innumerable
1. 無数の
2. 無理な
3. 無力の

(e)　disorder
1. 不足
2. 分離
3. 障害

(f)　imaginary number
1. 実数
2. 虚数
3. 素数

(g) storage device
$\left\{\begin{array}{l}\end{array}\right.$
1. 組込装置
2. 通信装置
3. 記憶装置

(h) duration
$\left\{\begin{array}{l}\end{array}\right.$
1. 耐久性
2. 微調整
3. 継続期間

(i) merchandise
$\left\{\begin{array}{l}\end{array}\right.$
1. 商品
2. 商人
3. 商業

(j) cell culture
$\left\{\begin{array}{l}\end{array}\right.$
1. 細胞結合
2. 細胞分裂
3. 細胞培養

Ⅱ　次の (a) から (j) の各日本語について、最適な英語を選び、その番号を解答欄に記入しなさい。

(a) 省略形
$\left\{\begin{array}{l}\end{array}\right.$
1. assimilation
2. acceleration
3. abbreviation

(b) 仮想の
$\left\{\begin{array}{l}\end{array}\right.$
1. focal
2. virtual
3. confidential

(c) 山形鋼
$\left\{\begin{array}{l}\end{array}\right.$
1. angle steel
2. hard steel
3. magnetic steel

(d) 塩素
1. sulfur
2. chlorine
3. hydrogen

(e) 接続
1. compensation
2. configuration
3. connection

(f) 汚染物質
1. antidote
2. pollutant
3. lubricant

(g) 吸込
1. suction
2. effusion
3. transition

(h) 衝突する
1. pervade
2. collide
3. extrude

(i) 静止軌道
1. space orbit
2. satellite orbit
3. stationary orbit

(j) 徹底的に
1. scarcely
2. concisely
3. thoroughly

Ⅲ　次の (a) から (d) の英語の説明に対応する語を下の 1 から 10 より選び、その番号を解答欄に記入しなさい。なお、1 から 10 は 1 回しか使えない。

(a) A precious yellow metallic element, highly malleable and ductile, and not subject to oxidation or corrosion

(b) A word that refers to a person, place, thing, event, substance, or quality

(c) A relationship between two amounts, showing how much larger one amount is than the other

(d) A mechanical device consisting of a revolving shaft with angled blades

1. ratio　　　　2. silver　　　3. range　　　4. accelerator

5. copper　　　6. propeller　　7. noun　　　8. gold

9. percentage　10. verb

Ⅳ　次の (a) から (d) の各組の英文が同じ意味になるよう、(　) に入れる
　　最適な語を下の 1 から 10 より選び、その番号を解答欄に記入しなさい。
　　なお、1 から 10 は 1 回しか使えない。

(a)　Recent electric appliances are equipped with a system that can
　　 detect and analyze a problem in themselves without assistance.

　　 Recent electric appliances are equipped with a system having a
　　 (　　　　) capability.

(b)　The recorded speed went beyond the standard operating speed
　　 by a huge margin.

　　 The recorded speed (　　　　) the standard operating speed by
　　 a huge margin.

(c)　Salt is required for animals to make their bodies work properly.

　　 Animals need salt for their bodies to (　　　　) properly.

(d)　The scientist has discovered a substance that easily changes
　　 into a gas at room temperature.

　　 The scientist has discovered a substance that is (　　　　) at room
　　 temperature.

1. form 　　　2. function 　　3. stable 　　　4. self-diagnosis

5. live 　　　6. equivalent 　7. self-recording 　8. volatile

9. cultured 　10. exceeded

V　次の (a) から (h) の英文を完成させる語として、最適なものをそれぞれの 1 から 4 より選び、その番号を解答欄に記入しなさい。

(a)　It is dangerous (1. to　2. for　3. that　4. which) fly a fighter jet without a G-suit.

(b)　(1. Mercury　2. Venus　3. Jupiter　4. Mars) is the fourth planet of the solar system.

(c)　This exercise will help to (1. retrieve　2. relieve　3. receive　4. repeat) your lower-back pain.

(d)　Blind people rely heavily on their (1. senses　2. scenes　3. scents　4. scenics) of touch and hearing.

(e)　Organic food began to appear in the US when people objected to using artificial (1. gene adhesive　2. intelligence　3. ingredients　4. flavoring pollution).

(f)　Treatment using placebos may help a patient (1. ignore　2. suppress　3. activate　4. neglect) his or her own natural painkilling system.

(g)　A lens (1. amplifies　2. modulates　3. bundles　4. refracts) light; the light changes its direction when it passes through the lens.

(h)　Many technologies exist in computer networking, and each technology has features that (1. distinguish　2. allow　3. convert　4. rationalize) it from the others.

Ⅵ　次の英文を読んで、各設問に答えなさい。

A research group tested technology to address airframe noise, or noise that is produced by non-propulsive parts of the aircraft, during landing. Researchers successfully combined several technologies to (①) a greater than 70 percent reduction in airframe noise. While porous concepts for landing gear fairings had been studied before, ② the group's design was based on extensive computer simulations to produce the maximum amount of noise reduction without the penalty of increasing aerodynamic drag. The landing gear cavity was treated with a series of chevrons near its leading edge, and a net stretched across the opening to alter airflow, aligning ③ it more with the wing.

(a) 英文に最も合う見出しを、次の1から4より選び、その番号を解答欄に記入しなさい。

1. Achievement of 70% Reduction in Non-propulsive Parts
2. Computer Simulations to Reduce Airplane Noise
3. Noise Reduction During Landing
4. Application of Cavity Technology into Airplane Noise Reduction

(b) (①) に入る最も適切な語句を次の1から4より選び、その番号を解答欄に記入しなさい。

1. result
2. make
3. multiply
4. achieve

(c) 下線部②と同じ意味を持つ文を次の 1 から 4 より選び、その番号を解答欄に記入しなさい。

1. 研究グループはコンピュータでシミュレーションを元にした設計と実際のモデルでは、空気抵抗の大きさがかなり違うことに気づいた。

2. 研究グループは何度もコンピュータでシミュレーションをし、空気抵抗を大きくせずに騒音を最大限減らす設計をした。

3. 研究グループはコンピュータシミュレーションを通し、空気抵抗を大きくすることと引き換えに騒音を最大限減らす設計を思いついた。

4. 研究グループは何度もコンピュータでシミュレーションをしたが、空気抵抗を大きくせずに騒音を最大限減らす設計はついに見つけられなかった。

(d) 下線部③の it が何を指しているかを次の 1 から 4 より選び、その番号を解答欄に記入しなさい。

1. noise
2. drag
3. chevrons
4. airflow

Ⅶ　次の (a) から (f) について、各和文の意味を表すように 1 から 7 を並べかえて英文を作り、3 番目と 5 番目にくる語の番号を解答欄に記入しなさい。

(a) 図書館には、ダウンロード可能な論文が多数あるが、ダウンロードできるのは一日に 3 つまでである。

The library has many downloadable papers, but you (1. day 2. three 3. per 4. to 5. can only 6. up 7. download).

(b) 太陽黒点の活動は地球の磁場に影響を及ぼし、通信障害を引き起こすことがある。

The activity of sunspots (1. and　2. the earth　3. can affect 4. cause　5. of　6. communication failures　7. the magnetic field).

(c) 安全のため、終業時退社する前に、PCの電源コードを抜いてください。

As a precaution, (1. the computer　2. at　3. you　4. unplug 5. before　6. go　7. home) the end of the day.

(d) イルカは様々な音を出し、互いにコミュニケーションをとる。

Dolphins (1. to　2. communicate　3. sounds　4. many　5. make 6. with　7. different) each other.

(e) 発酵とは、有機物に酵母菌を加えた際に発生する化学変化である。

Fermentation is a chemical change (1. yeast　2. organic substances 3. added to　4. when　5. that　6. occurs　7. is).

(f) 担当者が戻り次第、あなたに連絡を差し上げるように伝えます。

I will (1. in charge　2. as soon as　3. to　4. you　5. tell 6. the person　7. contact) she returns.

第 118 回 (2019. 1)

I　次の (a) から (j) の各英語について、最適な日本語を選び、その番号を解答欄に記入しなさい。

(a) precisely
1. 均等に
2. 機械的に
3. 精密に

(b) equator
1. 緯度
2. 赤道
3. 南半球

(c) interaction
1. 相互作用
2. 相互接続
3. 相互依存

(d) adjoin
1. 結合する
2. 通過する
3. 隣接する

(e) sterilization
1. 殺菌
2. 精製
3. 圧縮

(f) architecture
1. 等価
2. 建築
3. 伝搬

(g)　radiation　　　　　　　　1.　放射
　　　　　　　　　　　　　　　2.　増幅
　　　　　　　　　　　　　　　3.　蛍光

(h)　strengthen　　　　　　　　1.　動力化する
　　　　　　　　　　　　　　　2.　集中する
　　　　　　　　　　　　　　　3.　強化する

(i)　synthesis　　　　　　　　　1.　調和
　　　　　　　　　　　　　　　2.　分配
　　　　　　　　　　　　　　　3.　合成

(j)　insulator　　　　　　　　　1.　整流子
　　　　　　　　　　　　　　　2.　絶縁体
　　　　　　　　　　　　　　　3.　換気装置

Ⅱ　次の (a) から (j) の各日本語について、最適な英語を選び、その番号を解答欄に記入しなさい。

(a)　乗法　　　　　　　　　　　1.　multifunction
　　　　　　　　　　　　　　　2.　multiplex
　　　　　　　　　　　　　　　3.　multiplication

(b)　往復運動　　　　　　　　　1.　reciprocation
　　　　　　　　　　　　　　　2.　synchronization
　　　　　　　　　　　　　　　3.　factorization

(c)　問題解決　　　　　　　　　1.　drawing
　　　　　　　　　　　　　　　2.　troubleshooting
　　　　　　　　　　　　　　　3.　processing

(d)　過度の

1. obscure
2. acute
3. excessive

(e)　最適の

1. sizable
2. optimum
3. certified

(f)　指針

1. pointer
2. axis
3. instrument

(g)　腐蝕

1. friction
2. corrosion
3. diffusion

(h)　組成

1. proposition
2. composition
3. position

(i)　ひび

1. crack
2. strain
3. rust

(j)　欠如

1. interference
2. divergence
3. absence

Ⅲ 次の (a) から (d) の英語の説明に対応する語を下の 1 から 10 より選び、その番号を解答欄に記入しなさい。なお、1 から 10 は 1 回しか使えない。

(a) A pipe or hole that dirty water or waste fluids flow into

(b) An inspection of an object to detect faults without impairing the quality of the product

(c) The capability of a computer to perform operations similar to learning and decision-making in humans

(d) A surface-active agent used for cleansing

1. virtual reality
2. incineration
3. drain
4. extinguisher
5. nondestructive testing
6. ventilation
7. remote manipulation
8. detergent
9. artificial intelligence
10. underpass

Ⅳ　次の (a) から (d) の各組の英文が同じ意味になるよう、（　）に入れる最適な語を下の 1 から 10 より選び、その番号を解答欄に記入しなさい。なお、1 から 10 は 1 回しか使えない。文頭に来るべき語であっても先頭は小文字になっている。

(a)　　Make this manual less complex.

　　　（　　　　　）this mannual.

(b)　　Stem cells form a new organ through growth and division.

　　　Stem cells grow and（　　　　　）to form a new organ.

(c)　　When an alcohol is treated with a carboxylic acid, an ester is made.

　　　An ester is（　　　　　）by treating an alcohol with a carboxylic acid.

(d)　　The Building Standard Act was reviewed every time we experienced a large earthquake.

　　　（　　　　　）a large earthquake hit, the Building Standard Act was reviewed.

1. decide　　　　2. how　　　　3. dive　　　　4. amplify

5. produced　　　6. simplify　　7. divide　　　8. whenever

9. evaporated　　10. purify

138

V　次の (a) から (h) の英文を完成させる語として、最適なものをそれぞ
　　れの1から4より選び、その番号を解答欄に記入しなさい。

(a)　Impurities in a liquid can be eliminated by passing the liquid
　　(1. through　2. into　3. on　4. by) a filter.

(b)　Distillation is a way of separating a mixture into its components. It is
　　based on (1. accuracies　2. consistencies 3. changes　4. differences)
　　in the boiling points of the components.

(c)　Water that is taken from a river is (1. totally　2. truly　3. rarely
　　4. absolutely) pure enough to drink.

(d)　The microwave oven (1. devises　2. agitates　3. emits　4. damages)
　　water molecules inside food and causes friction, which heats the
　　food.

(e)　Almost all stars and planets, including the earth, are (1. spherical
　　2. cylindrical　3. irregular　4. variable) in shape because of
　　gravity.

(f)　(1. Accidentally　2. Simply　3. Obviously　4. Hardly) press the
　　button, and the package will be tied up with the string in less
　　than three seconds.

(g)　The fabric shields people (1. over　2. after　3. through　4. against)
　　electromagnetic radiation from cell phones and other electronic
　　devices.

(h)　Red blood cells not only carry (1. hydrogen　2. hemorrhage
　　3. oxygen　4. respiration) to cells but also remove carbon dioxide
　　from them.

Ⅵ 次の英文を読んで、各設問に答えなさい。

Have you ever heard of carnivorous plants? ① <u>This may be
surprising, but these plants eat tiny animals for food.</u> All plants need
sunlight and soil in order to survive. However, carnivorous plants
cannot live only on sunlight and soil. They must digest tiny animals
for extra food. The most famous example is the Venus flytrap, which
originally comes from North America. ② <u>It</u> catches flies in its mouth,
and even has what looks like (③)! This kind of plant is popular
because many people buy it to grow in their own homes. They hand-
feed the plant with living flies.

(a) 英文に最も合う見出しを、次の1から4より選び、その番号を解
答欄に記入しなさい。

1. Living without Sunlight and Soil

2. How to Grow the Venus Flytrap

3. The Origin of Carnivorous Plants

4. Hungry Plants

(b) 下線部①の和訳として最も適切なものを次の1から4より選び、
その番号を解答欄に記入しなさい。

1. 驚くべきことに、これらの植物は動物のように少量の食物を必要
とする。

2. 驚くかもしれないが、これらの植物はとても小さな動物を食べるのだ。

3. 驚くには値しないが、これらの植物はとても小さな動物を食用に
するのだ。

4. これらの植物がとても小さな動物に食用にされる、というのは驚
くべきことかもしれない。

(c) 下線部②は文中の何をさしているか、最も適切なものを次の1から4より選び、その番号を解答欄に記入しなさい。

1. the Venus flytrap
2. North America
3. tiny animals
4. extra food

(d) （　③　）に入る最も適切な語を次の1から4より選び、その番号を解答欄に記入しなさい。

1. eyes
2. noses
3. hands
4. teeth

Ⅶ　次の (a) から (f) について、各和文の意味を表すように1から7を並べかえて英文を作り、3番目と5番目にくる語の番号を解答欄に記入しなさい。ただし、文頭に来るべき語であっても（　）内では先頭は小文字になっている。

(a) 図を 25% に縮小してください。

(1. of　2. figure　3. reduce　4. the　5. to　6. its　7. 25%) original size.

(b) ガソリンの蒸気は空気より重いので、低い所に溜まりやすい。

The (1. air　2. is　3. of　4. heavier　5. vapor　6. gasoline 7. than), so it tends to lie low.

(c) 火星の重力は地球の重力の約三分の一である。

Gravity of (1. that　2. about　3. is　4. a　5. third　6. Mars　7. of)
the earth.

(d) 従来からあるディーゼル車が、低 CO_2 排出量と燃費の良さから見
直されている。

Conventional diesel vehicles (1. because　2. revalued　3. low
4. being　5. are　6. their　7. of) CO_2 emissions and good mileage.

(e) 1961 年に行われた最初の有人宇宙飛行は、わずか1時間50分の長
さだった。

The first manned space flight conducted (1. and　2. 1961　3. was
4. fifty minutes　5. in　6. one hour 7. only) long.

(f) インターネットは本来、軍事目的で開発されたが、今では人々が
情報やデータをなるべく自由に交換できるよう整備されている。

The Internet was originally developed for military purposes, but
now it is (1. to allow　2. to exchange　3. as　4. people　5. freely
6. information and data　7. organized) as possible.

技術英検
2級解答

ならびに工業英検3級解答

第133回技術英検2級　2023.11　解答

Ⅰ　(a) 1　(b) 3　(c) 3　(d) 2　(e) 2
　　(f) 2　(g) 2　(h) 2　(i) 3　(j) 3　　　　　　　30点

Ⅱ　(a) 4　(b) 8　(c) 7　(d) 10　(e) 3　　　　　20点

Ⅲ　(a) 2　(b) 3　(c) 4　(d) 4　(e) 4
　　(f) 1　(g) 1　(h) 1　(i) 4　(j) 1　　　　　　　40点

Ⅳ　(a) 8　(b) 2　(c) 4　(d) 10　　　　　　　　20点

Ⅴ　(a) 15　(b) 12　(c) 9　(d) 4　(e) 13　(f) 11　　30点

Ⅵ　(a) 2　(b) 2　(c) 1　(d) 1　　　　　　　　　24点

Ⅶ　(a)　4-1

All parts (6. in direct contact / 2. with / 4. the equipment / 7. must / 1. be / 5. made /3. of) stainless steel.

(b)　6-1

To set up this printer, (4. plug / 3. it / 6. into / 2. your computer / 1. and / 5. turn / 7. on) the power.

(c) 6-2

This phenomenon appears (7. only / 3. when / 6. the input power / 5. is / 2. greater / 4. than / 1. a) certain value.

(d) 4-5

The two companies modified their (6. license agreement / 3. slightly / 4. in / 1. response / 5. to / 7. the /2. changing) situation.

(e) 1-7

Visitors are not (4. allowed / 2. to enter / 1. the control room / 5. without / 7. being / 3. escorted / 6. by) a staff member.

(f) 1-7

Recent studies (5. suggest / 4. that / 1. underwater noise / 3. can directly / 7. harm / 2. whales / 6. by) damaging their hearing.

36 点

第132回技術英検2級　2023.6　解答

I　(a) 2　(b) 3　(c) 2　(d) 1　(e) 3
　　(f) 3　(g) 1　(h) 2　(i) 1　(j) 3　　　　　　　　　30点

II　(a) 2　(b) 9　(c) 6　(d) 4　(e) 1　　　　　　　　　20点

III　(a) 4　(b) 4　(c) 3　(d) 1　(e) 3
　　(f) 4　(g) 2　(h) 3　(i) 1　(j) 4　　　　　　　　　40点

IV　(a) 4　(b) 7　(c) 6　(d) 10　　　　　　　　　　　20点

V　(a) 12　(b) 9　(c) 3　(d) 11　(e) 5　(f) 7　　　　30点

VI　(a) 3　(b) 2　(c) 4　(d) 3　　　　　　　　　　　24点

VII　(a) 3-5

The IoT refers to (7. devices / 4. that / 3. share / 2. information / 5. with / 6. one another / 1. via) the Internet.

(b) 5-6

This warning device (4. will / 2. let / 5. cyclists / 7. know / 6. when / 3. a car / 1. is) coming up behind them.

(c) 7-4

The grant will (5. enable / 3. us / 7. to / 1. continue / 4. the development / 2. of / 6. our patented) AI technology.

(d) 1-4

Spacecraft (3. traveling / 6. far away / 1. from the sun / 5. use / 4. large / 7. solar panels / 2. to get) the electricity they need.

(e) 4-3

Laser rays that pass through (2.this /1.optical / 4.device / 7.are / 3. refracted / 6.and / 5.converge) at a point.

(f) 6-5

Birds must provide their bodies with (4.necessary / 1.energy / 6. while / 3. minimizing / 5.their / 7. body / 2. weight) to fly.

36 点

第131回技術英検２級　2023.1　解答

I　(a) 1　(b) 2　(c) 3　(d) 3　(e) 1
　　(f) 2　(g) 1　(h) 2　(i) 1　(j) 3　　　　　　　20点

II　(a) 2　(b) 3　(c) 3　(d) 1　(e) 3
　　(f) 2　(g) 3　(h) 1　(i) 2　(j) 1　　　　　　　20点

III　(a) 4　(b) 5　(c) 9　(d) 8　　　　　　　　　　20点

IV　(a) 2　(b) 6　(c) 4　(d) 8　　　　　　　　　　20点

V　(a) 4　(b) 3　(c) 2　(d) 4　(e) 1
　　(f) 3　(g) 2　(h) 3　　　　　　　　　　　　　40点

VI　(a) 2　(b) 4　(c) 1　(d) 3　　　　　　　　　　32点

VII　(a) 2-1

The team's goal is to (3. make / 5. the assembly / 2. of / 4. the device / 1. easier / 7. for / 6. their) customers.

(b) 5-2

The dust and gases spewed from a comet (1. form / 7. a tail / 5. that / 3. stretches / 2. away / 4. from / 6. the sun).

(c) 6-3

If you have pesticide products not in use, safely (7. dispose / 2. of / 6. the pesticides / 5. to / 3. protect / 1. living / 4. things) and the environment.

(d) 5-6

(3. Ensure / 1. that / 5. the / 7. motor / 6. has / 2. stopped / 4. before) removing the safety cover.

(e) 2-1

(7. Domestic / 3. production / 2. of / 5. eco-friendly / 1. cars / 6. showed / 4. a) 6% increase over last year.

(f) 1-4

The ozone layer absorbs (2. most / 7. of / 1. the / 3. harmful / 4. ultraviolet / 6. rays / 5. coming) from the sun.

48 点

第130回技術英検2級　2022.11　解答

Ⅰ　(a) 3　(b) 2　(c) 3　(d) 1　(e) 2
　　(f) 3　(g) 1　(h) 2　(i) 3　(j) 1　　　　　　　20点

Ⅱ　(a) 1　(b) 2　(c) 3　(d) 1　(e) 2
　　(f) 3　(g) 2　(h) 1　(i) 3　(j) 2　　　　　　　20点

Ⅲ　(a) 6　(b) 10　(c) 8　(d) 9　　　　　　　　　20点

Ⅳ　(a) 4　(b) 3　(c) 5　(d) 7　　　　　　　　　20点

Ⅴ　(a) 3　(b) 4　(c) 4　(d) 1　(e) 3
　　(f) 2　(g) 3　(h) 4　　　　　　　　　　　　40点

Ⅵ　(a) 1　(b) 4　(c) 3　(d) 1　　　　　　　　　32点

Ⅶ　(a) 6-1

Our bodies have a lot (7. of / 4. nerve / 6. endings, / 3. which / 1. respond / 5. to / 2. touch).

(b) 3-2

The air (6. intake / 5. of / 3. a / 7. jet / 2. engine / 4. is / 1. covered) when a plane will not be used for a long period.

(c) 7-2

Sunspots are areas (3. where / 1. the magnetic / 7. field / 4. is / 2. stronger / 6. than / 5. anywhere) else on the sun.

(d) 2-5

(4. peripheral / 6. equipment / 2. of / 7. a / 5. computer / 1. includes / 3. I/O devices) and storage.

(e) 1-2

A further investigation will reveal damage (3. that / 7. is / 1. invisible / 5. to / 2. the / 4. naked / 6. eye).

(f) 1-3

It is necessary to (7. / find / 5. out / 1. the / 4. root / 3. cause / 2. to / 6. develop) an effective countermeasure.

48 点

第129回技術英検2級　2022.6　解答

I　(a) 3　(b) 2　(c) 3　(d) 1　(e) 2
　(f) 3　(g) 1　(h) 3　(i) 1　(j) 1　　　　　20点

II　(a) 3　(b) 2　(c) 1　(d) 3　(e) 2
　(f) 1　(g) 3　(h) 2　(i) 1　(j) 2　　　　　20点

III　(a) 8　(b) 4　(c) 10　(d) 9　　　　　20点

IV　(a) 6　(b) 9　(c) 10　(d) 8　　　　　20点

V　(a) 1　(b) 4　(c) 1　(d) 2　(e) 3
　(f) 1　(g) 4　(h) 2　　　　　40点

VI　(a) 1　(b) 2　(c) 2　(d) 4　　　　　32点

VII　(a)　2-1

It is said (7. that / 3.fully / 2. autonomous / 5. cars / 1. will / 4. be / 6.available) in the near future.

　(b)　4-6

Snow is precipitation in the form of ice crystals (3. that / 2. originate / 4. in / 7. clouds / 6. when / 1. temperatures / 5. are) below the freezing point.

(c) 6-5

Seed germination is the process (7. through / 4. which / 6. seeds / 1. develop / 5. into / 3. new / 2. plants).

(d) 5-3

By washing hands and wearing masks, infections (6. can / 2. be / 5. prevented / 1. from / 3. spreading / 4. to / 7. others) to some extent.

(e) 1-7

This square pipe (6. is / 5. made / 1. of / 3. aluminum / 7. with / 2. a / 4. cross-section) of 25 mm by 50 mm.

(f) 7-6

(5. Liquid / 4. nitrogen / 7. may / 1. cause / 6. skin / 3. injury / 2. because) its temperature is extremely low.

48 点

第128回技術英検2級　2022.1　解答

I　(a) 2　(b) 2　(c) 1　(d) 1　(e) 1
　　(f) 2　(g) 3　(h) 3　(i) 2　(j) 1　　　　　　20点

II　(a) 2　(b) 2　(c) 3　　　　(d) 1　(e) 2
　　(f) 1　(g) 3　(h) 1および3 *　(i) 2　(j) 1　　20点

III　(a) 4　(b) 1　(c) 3　(d) 5　　　　　　　20点

IV　(a) 7　(b) 1　(c) 6　(d) 2　　　　　　　20点

V　(a) 3　(b) 4　(c) 1　(d) 4　(e) 2
　　(f) 3　(g) 1　(h) 4　　　　　　　　　　40点

VI　(a) 2　(b) 3　(c) 3　(d) 3　　　　　　　32点

VII　(a)　2-1

All (3. air valves / 4. open / 2. when / 7. the / 1. computer / 6. detects / 5. that) the air pressure is too high.

(b)　7-6

We still do not know how (3. the / 5. brain / 7. works / 4. and / 6. why / 2. we / 1. have) a sense of self-awareness.

(c) 1-2

The subsequent (6. investigation / 4. revealed / 1. that / 7. the crude oil / 2. had been / 5. discharged / 3. from) a small crack in a pipeline.

(d) 7-3

The weight of (2. an object / 5. varies / 7. depending / 1. on / 3. where / 6. it / 4. is) measured.

(e) 7-2

To reduce the production cost, the company (5. relocated / 3. its / 7. factories / 6. to / 2. places / 4. where / 1. the land) was inexpensive.

(f) 5-6

A competent designer (1. should / 7. have / 5. good / 2. drawing / 6. skills / 4. as / 3. well) as the ability to use CAD.

48 点

---

* II (h) は複数の選択肢 (1 および 3) が正解となり得たため、全員正解として採点いたしました。

第127回技術英検2級　2021.11　解答

I　(a) 3　(b) 1　(c) 2　(d) 2　(e) 1
　(f) 3　(g) 1　(h) 2　(i) 1　(j) 1　　　　20点

II　(a) 3　(b) 3　(c) 2　(d) 1　(e) 3
　(f) 3　(g) 1　(h) 2　(i) 3　(j) 2　　　　20点

III　(a) 7　(b) 5　(c) 9　(d) 8　　　　20点

IV　(a) 10　(b) 8　(c) 2　(d) 7　　　　20点

V　(a) 1　(b) 4　(c) 1　(d) 3　(e) 2
　(f) 4　(g) 1　(h) 1　　　　40点

VI　(a) 2　(b) 1　(c) 4　(d) 4　　　　32点

VII　(a) 5-4

This country's (7. emission / 6. regulations / 5. are / 1. stricter / 4. than / 2. those / 3. of) other countries.

(b) 2-1

Be sure (4. to / 6. leave / 2. a / 7. small / 1. gap / 5. between / 3. these) two parts during the assembly.

(c) 5-1

Today, technology (4. has / 3. made / 5. it / 7. easier / 1. to / 6. communicate / 2. with) other people around the world.

(d) 1-7

The day will soon (3. come / 5. when / 1. even / 4. ordinary / 7. people / 6. can / 2. enjoy) traveling in space.

(e) 5-1

More and more consumers choose to buy (2. cosmetics / 7. that / 5. have / 3. been / 1. developed / 6. without / 4. animal) testing.

(f) 1-5

Multiply (4. both / 6. sides / 1. of / 2. the / 5. equation / 7. by / 3. two) to find the value of x.

48 点

第126回技術英検2級　2021.6　解答

I　(a) 2　(b) 3　(c) 2　(d) 3　(e) 1
　　(f) 2　(g) 1　(h) 2　(i) 3　(j) 2　　　　　　　　20点

II　(a) 3　(b) 2　(c) 3　(d) 1　(e) 2
　　(f) 2　(g) 3　(h) 1　(i) 1　(j) 3　　　　　　　　20点

III　(a) 7　(b) 4　(c) 3　(d) 5　　　　　　　　　　20点

IV　(a) 3　(b) 5　(c) 2　(d) 7　　　　　　　　　　20点

V　(a) 1　(b) 4　(c) 3　(d) 4　(e) 2
　　(f) 4　(g) 1　(h) 1　　　　　　　　　　　　　40点

VI　(a) 3　(b) 2　(c) 1　(d) 1　　　　　　　　　　32点

VII　(a) 1-5

When the server went down, (6. everyone / 2. panicked / 1. because / 7. all the data / 5. could / 3. have /4. disappeared).

　(b) 1-2

This paper aptly (4. illustrates / 7. how / 1. a / 6. group / 2. of / 5. spheres / 3. behave) collectively under strong wind.

(c) 6-5

Scientists discovered that (4. these / 2. genes / 6. may / 7. be / 5. involved / 3. in / 1. causing) early heart disease.

(d) 3-4

The company decided to modify their products (2. in / 6. order / 3. to / 5. satisfy / 4. the / 7. needs / 1. of) new customers.

(e) 1-6

Over the next fifty years, (4. many / 7. human / 1. workers / 3. will / 6. be / 5. replaced / 2. by) robots and machines.

(f) 5-1

What will happen when (3. all / 6. the / 5. earth's / 4. fossil / 1. fuels / 7. are / 2. exhausted) in the future?

48 点

第125回技術英検2級　2021.1　解答

Ⅰ　(a) 1　(b) 3　(c) 3　(d) 2　(e) 2
　　(f) 2　(g) 3　(h) 1　(i) 3　(j) 3　　　　　　　20点

Ⅱ　(a) 3　(b) 3　(c) 3　(d) 3　(e) 2
　　(f) 2　(g) 3　(h) 3　(i) 2　(j) 1　　　　　　　20点

Ⅲ　(a) 3　(b) 7　(c) 4　(d) 8　　　　　　　　　20点

Ⅳ　(a) 9　(b) 5　(c) 6　(d) 2　　　　　　　　　20点

Ⅴ　(a) 1　(b) 4　(c) 2　(d) 4　(e) 1
　　(f) 1　(g) 4　(h) 1　　　　　　　　　　　　40点

Ⅵ　(a) 4　(b) 1　(c) 1　(d) 3　　　　　　　　　32点

Ⅶ　(a) 5-6

It is very difficult (3. to / 1. explain / 5. every / 2. scientific / 6. phenomenon / 7. solely / 4. through) physics.

(b) 1-3

The newly (2. developed / 6. control system / 1. can / 5. reduce / 3. energy / 7. use / 4. by) about 30%.

(c) 7-2

Some high-speed trains (3. have / 5. a / 7. maximum / 4. speed / 2. of / 6. more / 1. than) 300 km per hour.

(d) 1-7

There (5. is / 2. strong / 1. evidence / 4. that / 7. Mars / 3. was / 6. covered) with water 137 meters deep in ancient times.

(e) 4-7

Look for "https" at the beginning of a URL (5. to / 2. determine / 4. whether /1. the / 7. website / 3. is / 6. encrypted).

(f) 2-1

A sphere always appears to have a completely round (6. outline / 3. from / 2. wherever / 5. you / 1. look / 7. at / 4. it).

48 点

第124回技術英検2級　2020.11　解答

I　(a) 2　(b) 1　(c) 2　(d) 1　(e) 3
　　(f) 3　(g) 2　(h) 1　(i) 3　(j) 3　　　　　　　20点

II　(a) 1　(b) 2　(c) 2　(d) 3　(e) 1
　　(f) 2　(g) 2　(h) 1　(i) 3　(j) 3　　　　　　　20点

III　(a) 8　(b) 4　(c) 3　(d) 10　　　　　　　　20点

IV　(a) 8　(b) 9　(c) 2　(d) 3　　　　　　　　　20点

V　(a) 1　(b) 4　(c) 3　(d) 2　(e) 3
　　(f) 1　(g) 1　(h) 2　　　　　　　　　　　　　40点

VI　(a) 1　(b) 3　(c) 4　(d) 1　　　　　　　　　32点

VII　(a)　5-4

It is said (7. that / 3. skipping / 5. breakfast / 1. is / 4. unhealthy / 6. and / 2. can) cause weight gain.

(b)　3-1

The new aircraft is (7. so / 2. light / 3. and / 4. fuel-efficient / 1. that / 6. it / 5. will) be used in long-haul routes.

(c) 5-7

A heart transplant is considered one of the (6. most / 2. difficult / 5. surgeries / 1. and / 7. is / 4. performed / 3. under) extreme caution.

(d) 3-6

The total magnification of a microscope (2. is / 1. a product / 3. of / 4. the / 6. magnification of / 5. its / 7. individual) lenses.

(e) 2-7

A major problem (3. in / 5. the developing countries / 2. is / 1. to / 7. provide / 6. people / 4. with) safe drinking water.

(f) 1-6

The (3. mean / 7. is / 1. the / 4. sum / 6. of / 2. the numerical values / 5. divided) by the number of the values.

48 点

第122回工業英検3級　2020.1　解答

I   (a) 3   (b) 1   (c) 3   (d) 3   (e) 1
    (f) 2   (g) 3   (h) 3   (i) 3   (j) 2   20点

II   (a) 1   (b) 3   (c) 2   (d) 3   (e) 2
    (f) 3   (g) 2   (h) 3   (i) 1   (j) 2   20点

III   (a) 7   (b) 9   (c) 2   (d) 10   20点

IV   (a) 3   (b) 10   (c) 8   (d) 4   20点

V   (a) 1   (b) 3   (c) 4   (d) 3   (e) 1
    (f) 1   (g) 4   (h) 1   40点

VI   (a) 1   (b) 2   (c) 3   (d) 4   32点

VII   (a) 5-2

You can control (6. the speed of / 4. the pneumatic cylinder / 5. by / 7. adjusting / 2. the flow rate / 1. with / 3. a valve).

    (b) 3-2

This newly developed (6. scanner / 1. is / 3. much / 7. more / 2. user-friendly / 4. than / 5. the previous) model.

(c) 4-6

This study shows that (5. fatty / 7. diets / 4. are / 2. associated / 6. with / 3. a / 1. high) rate of heart disease.

(d) 3-5

The density of a material (4. is / 7. defined / 3. as / 1. its / 5. mass / 2. per / 6. unit volume).

(e) 5-7

The (4. funding / 3. for / 5. supercomputers / 2. fell / 7. behind / 1. other / 6. areas) of computer science.

(f) 7-5

Please keep (3. me / 6. informed / 7. of / 1. the status of / 5. the experiment / 4. you / 2. started) last week.

48 点

第121回工業英検3級　2019.11　解答

I　(a) 2　(b) 1　(c) 3　(d) 3　(e) 2
　(f) 3　(g) 3　(h) 2　(i) 3　(j) 1　　　　20点

II　(a) 1　(b) 3　(c) 3　(d) 3　(e) 2
　(f) 3　(g) 3　(h) 3　(i) 1　(j) 2　　　　20点

III　(a) 9　(b) 10　(c) 1　(d) 3　　　　20点

IV　(a) 4　(b) 5　(c) 3　(d) 6　　　　20点

V　(a) 4　(b) 3　(c) 3　(d) 4　(e) 1
　(f) 3　(g) 1　(h) 1　　　　40点

VI　(a) 4　(b) 4　(c) 4　(d) 3　　　　32点

VII　(a) 4-5

Could (7. you / 6. tell / 4. me / 1. who / 5. I / 3. should / 2. contact) if I find out that the parts do not fit?

(b)　7-6

This system automatically (4. saves / 5. inspection / 7. data / 1. to / 6. cloud storage / 3. at / 2. 15-minute) intervals.

(c) 1-6

The weather satellite (4. orbits / 3. the / 1. earth / 2. at / 6. a / 5. speed / 7. of) 1600 kilometers an hour.

(d) 7-3

Lead-acid batteries (6. are / 1. too / 7. heavy / 5. to / 3. be / 4. used / 2. in) electric vehicles.

(e) 1-2

The (5. diameters / 4. of / 1. these capsules / 6. vary / 2. in / 7. the range of / 3. 50 to 100) microns.

(f) 7-5

Heat (2. the flask / 4. so / 7. that / 3. water vapor / 5. will / 1. come / 6. out) of the opening.

48 点

第120回工業英検3級　2019.7　解答

I　(a) 3　(b) 3　(c) 2　(d) 2　(e) 1
　　(f) 2　(g) 3　(h) 1　(i) 3　(j) 2　　　　　　　　20点

II　(a) 3　(b) 2　(c) 3　(d) 2　(e) 2
　　(f) 2　(g) 1　(h) 1　(i) 3　(j) 3　　　　　　　　20点

III　(a) 7　(b) 9　(c) 6　(d) 1　　　　　　　　　　20点

IV　(a) 6　(b) 10　(c) 5　(d) 7　　　　　　　　　　20点

V　(a) 1　(b) 3　(c) 3　(d) 1　(e) 4
　　(f) 3　(g) 1　(h) 3　　　　　　　　　　　　　　40点

VI　(a) 4　(b) 2　(c) 1　(d) 3　　　　　　　　　　32点

VII　(a) 6-2

All (3. the / 7. refurbishments / 6. will / 4. have / 2. been / 5. completed / 1. by) the end of the year.

(b) 1-5

In the glass recycling process, glass is sorted by (7. color / 2. before / 1. it / 6. is / 5. washed / 4. to / 3. remove) impurities.

(c) 5-7

Many people (2. were / 1. not / 5. paid / 3. on / 7. time / 4. because / 6. of) the system error.

(d) 3-2

This tape will (4. lose / 5. its / 3. adhesiveness / 6. if / 2. exposed / 7. to / 1. sunlight) for a long time.

(e) 1-7

A translucent material (6. allows / 3. some / 1. light / 5. to / 7. pass / 2. through / 4. it).

(f) 6-4

Prior-art search (3. will / 7. help / 6. you / 5. decide / 4. whether / 2. to / 1. apply) for a patent or not.

48 点

第119回工業英検3級　2019.5　解答

I　(a) 3　(b) 2　(c) 3　(d) 1　(e) 3
　　(f) 2　(g) 3　(h) 3　(i) 1　(j) 3　　　　　20点

II　(a) 3　(b) 2　(c) 1　(d) 2　(e) 3
　　(f) 2　(g) 1　(h) 2　(i) 3　(j) 3　　　　　20点

III　(a) 8　(b) 7　(c) 1　(d) 6　　　　　　　　20点

IV　(a) 4　(b) 10　(c) 2　(d) 8　　　　　　　　20点

V　(a) 1　(b) 4　(c) 2　(d) 1　(e) 3
　　(f) 3　(g) 4　(h) 1　　　　　　　　　　　　40点

VI　(a) 3　(b) 4　(c) 2　(d) 4　　　　　　　　32点

VII　(a) 6-2

The library has many downloadable papers, but you (5. can only / 7. download / 6. up / 4. to / 2. three / 3. per / 1. day).

　(b) 5-1

The activity of sunspots (3. can affect / 7. the magnetic field / 5. of / 2. the earth / 1. and / 4. cause / 6. communication failures).

(c) 5-6

As a precaution, (4. unplug / 1. the computer / 5. before / 3. you / 6. go / 7. home / 2. at) the end of the day.

(d) 7-1

Dolphins (5. make / 4. many / 7. different / 3. sounds / 1. to / 2. communicate / 6. with) each other.

(e) 4-7

Fermentation is a chemical change (5. that / 6. occurs / 4. when / 1. yeast / 7. is / 3. added to / 2. organic substances).

(f) 1-7

I will (5. tell / 6. the person / 1. in charge / 3. to / 7. contact / 4. you / 2. as soon as) she returns.

48 点

第118回工業英検3級　2019.1　解答

I　(a) 3　(b) 2　(c) 1　(d) 3　(e) 1
　　(f) 2　(g) 1　(h) 3　(i) 3　(j) 2　　　　　　　20点

II　(a) 3　(b) 1　(c) 2　(d) 3　(e) 2
　　(f) 1　(g) 2　(h) 2　(i) 1　(j) 3　　　　　　　20点

III　(a) 3　(b) 5　(c) 9　(d) 8　　　　　　　　　　20点

IV　(a) 6　(b) 7　(c) 5　(d) 8　　　　　　　　　　20点

V　(a) 1　(b) 4　(c) 3　(d) 2　(e) 1
　　(f) 2　(g) 4　(h) 3　　　　　　　　　　　　　40点

VI　(a) 4　(b) 2　(c) 1　(d) 4　　　　　　　　　　32点

VII　(a)　2-7

(3. Reduce / 4. the / 2. figure / 5. to / 7. 25% / 1. of / 6. its) original size.

(b)　6-4

The (5. vapor / 3. of / 6. gasoline / 2. is / 4. heavier / 7. than /1. air), so it tends to lie low.

(c) 2-5

Gravity of (6. Mars / 3. is / 2. about / 4. a / 5. third / 1. that / 7. of) the earth.

(d) 2-7

Conventional diesel vehicles (5. are / 4. being / 2. revalued / 1. because / 7. of / 6. their / 3. low) CO_2 emissions and good mileage.

(e) 3-6

The first manned space flight conducted (5. in / 2. 1961 / 3. was / 7. only / 6. one hour / 1. and / 4. fifty minutes) long.

(f) 4-6

The Internet was originally developed for military purposes, but now it is (7. organized / 1. to allow / 4. people / 2. to exchange / 6. information and data / 3. as / 5. freely) as possible.

48 点

2024年度版技術英検 2 級問題集

2024 年 3 月 5 日 初版 第 1 刷発行

編著者―一般社団法人日本能率協会　JSTC 技術英語委員会
　　　　©2024 Japan Society for Technical Communication
発行者―張 士洛
発行所―日本能率協会マネジメントセンター
〒103-6009　東京都中央区日本橋 2-7-1　東京日本橋タワー
TEL 03（6362）4339（編集）／ 03（6362）4558（販売）
FAX 03（3272）8127（編集・販売）
https://www.jmam.co.jp/

装　丁―冨澤崇（EBranch）
印刷所・製本所―三松堂株式会社

本書の内容の一部または全部を無断で複写複製（コピー）することは、
法律で認められた場合を除き、著作者および出版者の権利の侵害となり
ますので、あらかじめ小社あて許諾を求めてください。

ISBN978-4-8005-9170-8 C3082
落丁・乱丁はおとりかえします。
PRINTED IN JAPAN

これなら通じる
技術英語ライティングの基本

これなら
通じる

Basics of
Technical
Writing

技術英語
ライティングの
基本

日本工業英語協会 専任講師
平野信輔 著
Shinsuke Hirano

▶▶▶ 誰にでも正確に伝わる!
第一線の技術翻訳者が教える
英文作成のコツ

日本能率協会マネジメントセンター

平野 信輔 著

本書は、工業・技術分野の情報を発信するときに必要となる、「正確」「明確」「簡潔」な英文を作成するための初歩的なポイントを解説する本です。解説の形式も先生と生徒の対話形式ですので、堅苦しくなく一人でも読み進めやすい、また間違えやすいポイントがわかりやすい内容となっています。英語の表記法であるパンクチュエーションの説明やミニコラムも充実しており、初学者にぴったりの一冊です。

●A5判　216頁

日本能率協会マネジメントセンター